NO OTHER WAY

Also By Charles North

Poetry

Lineups, 1972
Elizabethan & Nova Scotian Music, 1974
Six Buildings, 1977
Leap Year: Poems 1968-1978, 1978
Gemini, 1981 (with Tony Towle)
The Year of the Olive Oil, 1989
re: Chapbook 2, 1996 (with Elizabeth Robinson and Sianne Ngai)
New & Selected Poems, 1998

Editor

Broadway: A Poets and Painters Anthology, 1979 (with James Schuyler)
Broadway 2, 1989 (with James Schuyler)
Co-Editor, *The Green Lake Is Awake: Selected Poems by Joseph Ceravalo*, 1994

NO OTHER WAY

Selected Prose

CHARLES NORTH

Hanging Loose Press
Brooklyn, New York

Published by Hanging Loose Press, 231 Wyckoff Street, Brooklyn, NY 11217. All rights reserved. No part of this book may be reproduced without the publisher's written permission, except for brief quotations in reviews.

Printed in the United States of America
10 9 8 7 6 5 4 3 2 1

Many of these pieces, some in earlier versions, originally appeared in the following publications: *The Poetry Project Newsletter, Art in America, The World, L=A=N=G=U=A=G=E, Joe Soap's Canoe, American Book Review, Denver Quarterly, American Poetry Review, Pataphysics,* and *Lingo*; and in the anthologies *Out of This World*, edited by Anne Waldman (Crown, 1991), *That Various Field for James Schuyler*, edited by William Corbett and Geoffrey Young (The Figures, 1991), and *Ecstatic Occasions, Expedient Forms*, edited by David Lehman (Michigan University Press, 1996).

Cover art by Paula North

Library of Congress Cataloging-in-Publication Data

North, Charles.
   No other way : poets, critics, and painters / Charles North.
     p.   cm.
   ISBN 1-882413-53-9 (cloth). -- ISBN 1-882413-52-0 (paper)
    1. American poetry--20th century--History and criticism.
   2. Criticism--United States--History--20th century. 3. Painting.
American. I. Title.
   PS323.5.N67   1998
811'.5409--dc21   97-46108
                                   CIP

 Produced at The Print Center, Inc., 225 Varick St., New York, NY 10014, a non-profit facility for literary and arts-related publications. (212) 206-8465

Contents

III.

AUTHOR'S NOTE

The pieces collected here are occasional, in both senses. Most came about by invitation. In a few instances, I was stimulated (or provoked) enough to write something on my own. In putting the manuscript together, I tried to avoid the temptation to rewrite, as opposed to occasionally clarifying or smoothing out—especially strong in the case of pieces 20 years old and more. This has meant living with a certain amount of unease, for example, at the tone of my early piece on Harold Bloom reading John Ashbery—the same Harold Bloom who has been one of literature's staunchest defenders against those who would reduce it to something else.

The arrangement is mostly chronological.

Do not

frighten me more than you
have to!

—*Frank O'Hara*

I

LIFE IN (MIS-)PRISION

Here goes. Two years ago I read a highly laudatory article on John Ashbery by the critic Harold Bloom (*Salmagundi*, Spring-Summer 1973) which left me unexpectedly dismayed. In the piece Bloom called Ashbery one of the two strongest poets "in mid-career" (the other being Ammons) and "something close to a great poet." On the face of it that seems wonderful. Here was an influential critic at Yale welcoming one of the most striking members of the avant-garde (and a poet revered, I don't think that's too strong a word, by younger experimental poets all over) into the pantheon while still "in mid-career." The problem was, and continues to be, the reasons for the acceptance, in fact the critical approach: one designed, it seems to me, not only to turn off anyone who might really be interested in contemporary poetry but to do an important disservice to all concerned, Ashbery, poets, poetry, even criticism.

Bloom makes some interesting points in the article, which is heroic given the difficulty of the poetry; though he never manages to say exactly why Ashbery is one of the privileged "strong" poets (other than to hold him up tautologically as an exemplar of the

[*Poetry Project Newsletter*, March 1976]

underlying theory). He speaks perceptively of Ashbery's "tacitly rejecting a poetry of privileged moments or phrases," and he also shows savvy (however couched in academic jargon) in dealing with particular poems like "Clepsydra," which he describes as sitting "on the page as a forbiddingly solid wall of print...turning a Shellyan-Stevensian self-referential quality into an absolute impasse." But characteristically he manages to subvert, if not swamp, the praise with one of the most elaborated (*not* elaborate) critical apparatuses to appear in modern times. The keynote of Bloom's approach, expounded at great length in *The Anxiety of Influence* and sequels, is the idea that so-called strong poets unconsciously misread ("misprision" is his term), "swerve away from," even kill off their poetic fathers as a matter of poetic survival. It's certainly an intriguing idea—unless you happen to be violently anti-Freudian. (If it's all unconscious, how can you dispute it?) But it begins quickly to seem a truism. Staking out territory is every poet's survival problem almost by definition, and being influenced and then transforming or shedding the influence, sometimes consciously, is one of the motor activities beneath every poetic "career" (which word, as in "mid-career," I realize has been annoying me. Did Keats have a mid-career? Rimbaud? I'm "between careers."). That doesn't mean that either poetry or individual poems can be reduced to influence-anxiety. It does mean that once the gun is loaded, there are innumerable opportunities to fire it, regardless of how helpful or wrong-headed or tiresome that may be.

With such a "serious" notion of poetry, it isn't surprising that Bloom's aim is directed at what is—what looks—serious. (The look of seriousness is a little like "The Look of Love," it can make you turn off your radio.) If your method is primarily conceptual, then you spend your time with what can be conveniently conceptualized (*not* "The Grapevine," not "Leaving the Atocha Station," not "Europe"). And you spend your time, or most of it, paraphrasing or theme-tracing. Of course there's nothing wrong with those activities in themselves; they can be helpful. Ashbery, after *The Tennis Court Oath*, does deal in concepts, and he is serious and difficult (although perhaps not as difficult as he can be made to seem). The nuances of feeling that are worked through in "The System," for example, require study, not just reading. But all good poets (like so many bad ones) are serious, even the funniest or seemingly most frivolous. (Once when the poet Larry Fagin showed me a new manuscript of his, I quipped, "You're getting serious!" To which he properly replied, "I'm *always* serious.") The point is that poets aren't serious only when they look it; nor are they necessarily or only at their best then.

Another thing I have a feeling Bloom does—and it seems strange to say it—is pay too much attention to Ashbery the explicator of his own poems, the author who steps in like the narrator of an old-fashioned novel to tell us what he is or isn't doing (doubly strange in that Bloom's book is dedicated to W.K. Wimsatt—whatever happened to the "intentional fallacy"?). Ashbery's poetry is filled with talk and some of the talk certainly is about the poetry itself. But the self-deflations, the undercutting, even the explanations can't, it seems to me, be taken at face value. The tone is too wry, the self-consciousness (artistic) too acute. Often the overt subject matter seems more of a screen, far from all that is there. The "explications" are like tracks made with snowshoes: there's too much underneath, they're too much of the moment, for a reader to be satisfied with them. If there is a genuine apology at any point, as, for example, towards the close of Part I of "The Skaters," the best bet, I think, is to take it as modesty, perhaps even momentary insecurity; brilliance,

11

after all, is no defense against anxiety. But Ashbery is no more *sorry* about what he's written than Williams was about eating the plums—or than we are. "Mild effects" indeed. For a critic with one foot in the unconscious to be led, to this degree, by the conscious in the poetry is too convenient.

Bloom canonizes Ashbery's "putting it all in" from "The Skaters" on—in *The Tennis Court Oath* he left it all out, though the "it" tersely enough tells what Bloom somehow won't see—primarily the banalities, the clichés. But the putting-in strategy goes for ideas as well, which ups the ante tremendously. Ashbery might be called, at least partly, a surrealist of the intellect: it is ideas as much as images which are allowed to spill out as images do in dreams, which is tantamount to a total trusting of the unconscious. There is, moreover, a kind of snowball effect in which each discovery seems to beget new ones: unconscious and conscious fuse into something like an extended epiphany—which paradoxically resists explanation. It is almost as if Ashbery were playing with ideas emotionally or sensuously as a child might, rather than conceptually which we assumed was the only way, and accepting the inevitable mysteries resulting from such a procedure. That the result is both emotionally and conceptually rich despite being "unedited" is his genius. This way of working, it occurs to me, is related to his overt use of collage throughout. In "collaging" from himself, he makes explicit what is operating undercover when he uses material from children's books, newspapers, etc., namely the role of the unconscious. At the very least he makes things far too complex for the usual exegesis; there is simply too much mingling of truths, half-truths, truisms, heard remarks, philosophical speculation, folksy wisdom, cornball nonwisdom, etc. He's too willing to write anything.

In fact it strikes me that Ashbery is one of the most self-indulgent writers who ever lived. Can you imagine writing this, and letting it stand unrevised?

> Leading liot act to foriage is activity
> Of Chinese philosopher here on Autumn Lake
>> thoughtfully inserted in
> Plovince of Quebec
>> ["On Autumn Lake"]

Similarly, six lines into the long, marvelous and very serious poem "Grand Galop," a dopey school lunch menu is allowed to materialize, replete with sloppy joes, scalloped corn, all those things we used to lump together in school as shit on toast. "On Autumn Lake" is not Ashbery's best poem—"Grand Galop" is close—but it is, I think, one of the clues to his brilliance. He fools around. He lets all manner of things into print. He continually does what you're not allowed to do. Of course it doesn't work every time. But by trusting himself absolutely, by indulging himself, seeing what's really inside—he is able to arrive at those illuminations that seem to abound in his poems. In "Autumn Lake" he tells himself: "stop it!" Then: "I will not." And that's that, it stays. Bad taste? Horrible. But it's emblematic: here, as elsewhere, the willingness to write *anything* is a virtual modus operandi.

As far as the leaving out goes, the mode of *The Tennis Court Oath,* Bloom's outright dismissal seems to me a selective blindness. (Why, it's hard not to wonder, would he analyze the reductive impulse in modern poetry in general, and be unwilling to acknowledge fragmentation and ellipsis in particular?) The disjunctive, the non-discursive in general, and the non-earnest seem somehow to elude (annoy?) him. I think he misses the disjunction in the more recent poems too, where it is masked by the pervading discursive tone—almost as if he would close the significant gaps by force. And the Great Tradition, or its current version, rolls on, stretched a bit to accommodate Ashbery, but not really changed over as it should be by one of the masters of 20th-century art. Or (to stabilize the metaphor), the critical mill keeps turning, satisfied for the moment, certain to be unhappy an hour later, and in the meantime finding more undigested morsels than it bargained for or can even acknowledge.

Wasn't the positive contribution of the New Critics, for all their tunnel vision, to bring attention back to the poem? I guess, finally, that's what has been bothering me most. With the laying on of influence theory, the poetry—contemporary poetry, what we're all interested in—seems a kind of poor relation, understood when it is really looked at (though too often through academic glasses) but more often the vehicle for whatever it is the critic needs to get off his/her chest. It becomes an excuse and no more. As if the difficulty, the modernism Bloom (and, to be fair, a great many other critics) sees were merely a tic—or worse, something perverse, put in the way of the critic to make it hard for him to get down to the *ideas* that matter. So that Bloom's avowed hope for a more workable practical criticism seems to me ultimately ironic. However interesting his theory may be to structuralists or other combatants of criticism, he's not really dealing with the work of art. As idolatrous as his praise is at times, it hides its reasons for being so.

It occurred to me on first reading the *Salmagundi* article that there is a principle at work in reading poetry. I thought to call it the Attention Principle, on the idea that attention of a certain kind, when, paradoxically, it is too professional, too earnest, too "aggressive," produces a Heisenberg swerving of the poem away from the

14

reader: in certain instances, the more erudition the bigger the swerve. Maybe I mean the Humility Principle.[1] In the case of Ashbery, to miss the humor, the pervasive parody, the sheer play which generates so much else, is to miss the mark, *hamartia*. (Bloom's nomenclature is catching.) And since Bloom's shtick is the anxiety of influence, influence per se becomes the heavy—along, unfortunately, with Wallace Stevens, who is thrown at us with such persistence that *we* begin to want to kill him off. What is at first a promising insight, and is then elaborated into a dragnet—it's really a one-joke show for all its spinning out—ends by so overloading the poems that one wonders if anybody who hasn't already, will have the courage to read them.

As far as Ashbery's personal influence-anxiety is concerned, Stevens (and through him Whitman) becomes the efficient cause, the poetic father. Which of course makes sense. Ashbery, like other poets of his generation, *was* influenced by Stevens, who is a great poet and who needed to be swerved away from if Ashbery wasn't to be merely a disciple. It makes additional sense when you consider Stevens' seriousness, his elevated subject matter. Like frequently engenders like, though here the like is the poetry and the like is the criticism. Ashbery was also influenced by Raymond Roussel and John Cage (as importantly, I think, as by Stevens); by Auden, de Chirico, Mallarmé, Reverdy (I'm guessing a little), Rilke, Wheelwright, Marianne Moore, Eliot, Henry Green, Henry James...maybe Henry Green is his poetic uncle, then de Chirico could be the poetic godfather? Ashbery has done things Stevens didn't dream of doing, as far as I know, which isn't to take away from Stevens but which is to make reducing Ashbery to a particular survival swerve less than illuminating. Undoubtedly Ashbery picked up prose tone from Stevens (Auden, Eliot, etc.), but the changing of the terms of

15

discourse, the dead ends, misdirections, non sequiturs are as much from the others, who of course are outside the particularly American Tradition. Ashbery gets sidetracked and the sidings are as interesting as the terminus, are in fact ends in themselves. Which certainly adds to the mystery, but somehow doesn't detract from the emotional resonance. The paraphrasable content, it is curious to have to insist, isn't all that's going on. In a real sense Ashbery is the post-modern and Stevens the modern. Stevens even begins to seem traditional with his reiterations and iambic pentameter, for all his art about art. (As Leo Steinberg said of Jasper Johns: he forces you to lump Franz Kline and de Kooning with Rembrandt and Giotto).

Ashbery virtually changes the terms of the avant-garde by remaining there, a prime reason being that he is always outstripping himself as well as his poetic ancestors. He doesn't—as I think Bloom and, essentially, Stevens do—continue to draw the interest on an original way of working, an initial discovery. He transforms the poetic capital continually. Or rather, he transforms base materials into capital and then, since his poetic resources are so numerous, can keep drawing on capital. Among the poems in which he transforms "conventional" writing are "Idaho" (narrative structure, pulp fiction), "Into the Dusk Charged Air" (almanac language, development), "Farm Implements and Rootabagas in a Landscape" (subject matter, forms, tone), "Rivers and Mountains" (continuity, unlikely sources): all the ways, and there are loads more, one is not supposed to use language if one is aiming to be a serious poet. Bloom, seeing the poet's dilemma of finding out what's left to be done, doesn't accept the genuine discoveries once they are made. In the fifties when Ashbery began, one of the things left to do was to leave out. In the climate of serious, high-toned and academic verse that had poetry gasping for air, it was left to be anti-academic and irreverent like the poets in California and at Black Mountain and anti-academic and irreverent like the poets in New York. It was left, as well, to fool around, to include humor, to see what could conceivably emerge in the process of making a poem, rather than merely to receive or pre-form.

★ ★ ★

It appears to be the rule, of late, that interesting poets shy away from the business of literary criticism. (David Shapiro comes to mind as an exception; see his illuminating piece on Ashbery in *Field,* Fall 1971.) Maybe poets nowadays are particularly aware of the unconscious sources of their strengths and unwilling to risk proximity either to the poetry of others or to their own rationality, for fear the unconscious material will draw back and hide (like, pardon the expression, getting dried mucus out of a baby's nostril— you really have to wait for the sneeze to come). And since poetry came out of the *schools* in the fifties, it's been reluctant to go back.

It's unfair of me, I acknowledge, to make Bloom bear the weight of my pique regarding approaches to poetry, and he'll clearly survive it. In these same academic circles he is refreshingly maverick. But by perpetuating the primacy of everything *surrounding* the poetry, he is, I am afraid, working to close the windows again, to undermine the real gains. And to further Freudianize us, rather than leaving us to do that for ourselves (which we may all do sooner or later) is to extend the dragnet throughout space until things get pretty claustrophobic—while the poems themselves remain essentially closed off, at best intriguing. Although there are some important exceptions, the writings of Hugh Kenner for example, I have a feeling, perhaps partly wishful, that lit. criticism has some catching up to do not only with contemporary poetry but with the best art criticism, the kind that really looks at and grapples with the art and doesn't let psychology or history have (lose) its head. If Ashbery exemplifies certain unavoidable truths about all of us, or about all poets, well, then, he does. But he is also doing things in poems such as "Self-Portrait in a Convex Mirror" and *Three Poems* which are so varied, so new, that they require the very best attention. Assuring him a place in the tradition in Bloom's way is better, surely, than overlooking him (the all-too-familiar fate of innovators), but, ironically, it is also like D. H. Lawrence and the snake at his water trough: a missed opportunity of a momentous sort. A misprision.

---

[1] We don't, after all, really know how poetry (or painting or music) works on us, although we like to think so, particularly when we are attempting to write critically. Describing formal characteristics, or one's own responses, strictly speaking doesn't approximate the work of art—it only makes visible certain ways we have learned to talk about art. It's like being absolutely knocked out by a show of paintings and trying to make someone else understand why. You can talk a great deal, and talk well, but the gulf between the paintings and the talk is absolute. Moreover the terms of the praise often apply to art that doesn't mean nearly as much to you. This is by no means to allege that criticism is futile, but it is to suggest that overconfidence can be self-defeating, and that developing this or that set of meanings out of this or that poem is at best a clever, helpful paraphrase, and at worst a thorough distortion or reduction or both. Even with the well known anthology poems, the real reasons some move us to tears (Cf. "So we'll go no more a-roving," Wyatt's "They flee from me," "I know a bank where the wild thyme grows"), or whatever,

exist beneath and apart from conceptualizing. The textbook terms apply, music, image, association, idea, but their effect in concert, in the poem, remains unutterable. Art, at least as this goes to press, is still magical. The point is that criticism has shaky ground to operate on, but better shaky than papier-mâché, better to fumble around and dig out possibilities and be aware they're that, than to be content with systems.

Richard Tuttle: Small Pleasures

Richard Tuttle's work, seen in bulk for the first time in a retrospective at the Whitney, seems to find its champions and its detractors and not too many in between. Identified usually as a "post-Minimal" artist with Conceptual overtones, Tuttle has been working for more than 10 years in what appears, in hindsight, to have been a consistent direction, but which at each new stage was quite mystifying. There was the sense all along of an artist who was "onto something," possibly something important, but many viewers were at a loss to account for the presence and authority of what seemed at bottom extremely small gestures, like a series of almost invisible shapes of white paper (irregular octagons) pasted to the wall or hard-to-see pencil lines on the plaster with small pieces of wire nailed over them. Nor could the "theme" around which Tuttle was apparently creating his variations be located.

In the Whitney show, samples of each of Tuttle's stylistic periods—a retrospective for a 34-year-old artist makes the periods as minimal as the works—were allotted an extremely generous amount of open space. Given the low visibility of many of them, it might seem that the artist and the show's organizer, Marcia Tucker, were throwing down the gauntlet in a Dada spirit. But Tuttle, who has been centrally concerned with the environment of his works and has both fitted and created pieces in relation to specific exhibi-

[*Art in America,* November-December 1975]

tion spaces, has made it work. In keeping, too, with the impermanent aspect of his art, provision was made for him to change the pieces at intervals within each stylistic group (this goes to press after only the first installation). The groups included, in addition to the paper octagons and wire pieces, small paper cubes with variously shaped volumes ingeniously cut out of them, simple wood-relief shapes painted a single color, small alphabet-like objects of hollow galvanized tin, dyed-cloth octagons, string configurations on the floor (carpet) and plywood slats nailed to the bottom of the wall. There was also a roomful of drawings.

Carter Ratcliff has noted (*Art International*, May 1970) apropos the paper octagons, that Tuttle is concerned with esthetic quality, a concern that separates him from many other artists of his period. One has the impression that for all their contrariness and casualness, Tuttle's works are not, finally, Duchampian challenges; nor is their content exhausted once the concept is recognized. Even those pieces that seem meant to be funny (and there are many) aren't merely funny. The paper octagons—of which only one was in the first installation—exemplify this intangible resonance which convinces one that Tuttle matters as an artist. The one in the show (from 1970) was drawn in pencil, then cut out and pasted to the wall so its outline nearly disappeared. Though slightly creamier in color than the wall, reflecting more light, it was really a piece of the wall itself, a genuine ambiguity, as solid as fresco but as temporary as the exhibition. It seemed, as well, to open a hole in the white space and at the same time to crystallize space; its form was as mysterious—and touching—as dream shapes, with a similar sense of something completely beyond us, but central to us as well. What can account for that numinous quality? There is a suggestion here, certainly, of the magical objects of Surrealism. In Tuttle, however, the

21

influence of Surrealism is almost entirely abstracted, denatured; the work tempts one with possible allusions (to batiks for instance, in the cloth pieces) but denies one the comfort of anything really recognizable.

Tuttle's paper octagons represent a motif within his oeuvre. Before doing them, he had produced similar simple shapes in cloth, each dyed a different color. The dyeing was seemingly quite casual; in parts it looks faded. Each shape was hemmed on all sides but the hemming was ragged. (Why hem them?) Wrinkles in the cloth made it seem as if the pieces had been pulled out of a bin somewhere and stuck onto the wall, without any thought for how they would "look" (the *artist* not caring how they would look). Yet the tension between formal, contained shape and frayed, faded, rumpled fabric, as well as the natural topography of the folds with their shadows and highlights, held one's interest. The ones in the Whitney show, two octagons and an irregular horseshoe, had substantial echoes of the primitive, and where they curled away from the wall there was darkness and space behind, so that what would be dismaying in a dressmaker's shop or perhaps at a tapestry dealer's here had intriguing overtones. Tuttle's flattened shapes are clearly related to his reliefs: in all he seems to be confusing, on purpose, painting and sculpture, creating three-dimensional things but making them only minimally three-dimensional, so the idea of "thick painting" is there too. Seen from this angle, the progression of his work from paper cubes to wood and then tin reliefs, to cloth and then paper, constitutes a gradual destruction of space through flattening. One might expect the next step to be painting itself, where space is an illusion, or where it is no thicker than the paint. But in 1972 Tuttle shifted again, creating those mysterious pieces of wire and penciled wall-line that could be seen as sculpture or drawing or both.

Tuttle calls them simply wire pieces. Drawing the lines on the wall first, he nails one end of a very thin piece of wire to one end point of the line, then either lets the other end go free or nails it to the other end of the line. The wire invariably springs or twists into an interesting configuration, forming relationships with both the pencil line and the shadows cast by the wire on the wall. (Is the wire punning or "commenting" on the drawing? the shadow on the wire?) Tuttle has said that the process of making his works is a part of them, and one does feel the perverse recoiling of the wire, after it has been nailed and carefully stretched along the pencil line, to its final convolutions. It is hard to conceive of a small procedure with ramifications as wide. Tuttle's *20th Wire Piece,* 1972, starting from a scissor-like pencil line, became in addition a looping wire and, as a bonus, some shadowy drooping buttocks on the wall. In *6th Wire Bridge,* 1971, three very thin, roughly parallel wires of uneven length produce double and triple shadows, a fragile "tunable" lyricism (breathing on it set it in motion, like one of the old Aeolian harps).

10 Kinds of Memory and Memory Itself, 1973, punning inventively on tying a string around one's finger, was a pattern of pieces of white string laid on the Whitney's dark rug. The configurations managed to suggest the plan for a treasure hunt with all its misdirections—or one for a bombing raid which fortunately had been sabotaged. Clearly the work could not survive a breeze (or the vacuum cleaner), but it or its idea could be repeated. Here, too, whether there is three-dimensionality—whether the string is solid or just white line—is moot. Tuttle's other efforts in this direction— the tyranny over the large by the very small—included a two-inch piece of whitewashed rope pinned near the bottom of a large wall; two joined and overlapping bars of bright red paint at the outside corner of a wall; a tiny equilateral triangle of white paper, easily

23

missed. Tuttle's wit was evident in the drawings, two of which were titled *Paper Clip Tracing on Map Fragment* and *Stacked Colors,* and also in the paper cubes (from 1964) which, ingenious in design alone, looked like architectural models by an architect who chose to forget that people walk upright, can't fly, and are more important than buildings; and in the tin relief shapes, suggestive of scrap-metal cookie cutters.

It is difficult to say whether Tuttle appears at his best in a retrospective such as this or in individual shows where the full evocativeness of each piece can be sensed without the aroma of Dada. Since his work reverberates, comments, from one piece to the next and from one show to another, from large to small, solid to evanescent, serious to jokey, it does gain something definite from being seen en masse. One of the contradictions seemingly inherent in reductive art of all kinds is that in forcing viewers to pay attention to all that is there, the artist may encourage them—since the "all" is generally next to nothing—to see more than is there. But in Tuttle's case the all, fleeting as it first appears, is mysteriously illimitable, so his efforts, mediating between reference and non-reference, lyrical in addition to being intellectually challenging, are especially worth our attention.

WILD PROVOKE OF THE ENDURANCE SKY

Joseph Ceravolo's poetry has been appearing here and there, though not very frequently, since the publication of *Spring in This World of Poor Mutts* (Columbia U. Press, 1968), the first winner of the Frank O'Hara Award. His poems are and have been among the freshest, the most interesting, and the loveliest around. His voice is unlike anyone else's, a combination of extreme dislocation and disjunction of language with pure lyric. The combination is unique, close to paradoxical, yet the poems manage to be completely convincing. This is an early one:

A SONG OF AUTUMN

A dog disappears
across a small lake.
It waits for me.
It goes where I want to go.
Begins to wake up the flowers.
So leave us alone.
Because no freedom can choose
between faces and
hours as destroyed as moving,
or cold water in the

[*The World*, July 1976]

sun. I can go out
now and measure
the flies that swing around trees
like doctors around a woman
full of bars and beauties
you could never make free;
Not even if the
flowers turn to moss and
loose sensations for their stems.

Ceravolo's poems strike one as intensely personal, despite their modernist strategies. Many are gentle, intimate, about love, sex, family, weather, sadness, change, together with a sense of the cosmic forces that weave through and around all of these. Their riskiness in terms of language makes their success all the greater. His titles, which are like no one else's, suggest some of the marvelous, difficult-to-pin-down qualities of the poetry: "The Green Lake is Awake," "Fill and Illumined," "Passivation," "Wild Provoke of the Endurance Sky."

I think a part of his strength as a poet may derive from his other life as an engineer (or else relate to that part of him which is related to being an engineer). Despite the presence of so much *feeling* in his poetry, there is also a kind of rigor—coupled with a modesty, a tentativeness akin to Keats' "negative capability"—which ensures: no sloppiness, no dishonesty. How about this for a beginning:

There's nothing to love in this
rice Spring.

["Warmth"]

26

Or:

> I can't live blossoming drunk
>> ["The Book of Wild Flowers"]

Here is a recent poem, one of eight printed in *Big Sky* 9:

ANNUAL PARALLAX

The sun is in the sky
and it is bright.
The signs are bright
and soon there is something
to shine. Until the flower
coming out of the soil.
There is something dark
in this bright sun.
It is not my feeling toward
you; the universe; or feelings
of Spring.

Ceravolo's more recent poems, those that I've seen, are less severely dislocated syntactically and grammatically than his very early ones. But the marvelous childlike directness and wonder—he is the Master of the Quietly Blunt Question—are still there. The voice goes wherever it goes, by whatever it is led, logic or not. The poems should be set to music if they haven't been already; his major mode is pure, if distinctly modern, song. They should also be collected again, it's more than high time. Because it's a pleasure to copy them, and because they should be read above all, here are two more from his O'Hara Award-winning book.

PASSION FOR THE SKY

You are near me. The night
is rectilinear and light
in the new lipstick
on your mouth and on the colored
flowers. The irises are blue.
As far as I look we are across. A
boat crosses by. There is no monkey in me
left: sleep. There is something
sold, lemons. Corn is whizzing from the
ground. You are sleeping
and day starts its lipstick.
Where do we go from here?
Blue irises.

DATA

To indicate is to
turn off   in a world
away from ease.
Rotating in a mean format of oxygen.
First make and then
made all alone until
the end of a blank.
The smoke opens up and out
comes a word
in a new storage of love.
Turning off or
turning on the calcareous bases

we find our selves in
are set there by IT.
Divine and more
divine each day, no control,
but in another world.

TWO PAINTERS OF THE MEDITERRANEAN

1. Aristodemos Kaldis

A Kaldis landscape is like an overloaded closet, but the pleasures of what is likely to topple on you more than make up for the blow. Kaldis is a heady painter. In his recent show, his first in a decade, the sheer drops of Greek hills, the precariousness of tiny hilltop churches and houses, the jumble of people, animals, vegetation, boats, both in and out of scale, produce something like the lyrical vertigo of climbing a real Greek hill in a crowded Greek bus. If the classic Greek mind was partly a response to an unruly topography, both mind and topography have a champion here. At first glance Kaldis looks naif: the palette is full and bright, the content is at least partly mythological, the scale is inconsistent. But the confusion is a knowing one. Depicted things adjoin pure paint; a sea monster has a gleam in its eye that is too agreeable for us to be either frightened or condescending; there is visual punning that reveals a 20th-century artist who knows exactly what he is about, probably smiling behind the curtain of myth and sunlight.

In *Minerva Surveying While Europa Marches On,* 1974-1975, a landscape divided horizontally by water rises in flattened "primitive" space while a ghostly fantasy form (Minerva?) watches the proceedings from the top right—she's just an outline around white

[*Art in America,* May-June 1976; July-August 1977]

canvas (with one eye further whited out), to suggest all sorts of mythological possibilities, among them a twilight of mythology. Only on second glance do we see that the near shore is shaped into a giant bull's head and body, and that the tiny church on a hilltop is on the bull's hump. There is also the distinct possibility that a giant breast is entering the painting from the right, behind a giant orange nipple. Greece, after all, is fundamentally a fairyland, to which her real air and colors and her dream of the good life (periodically rudely awakened) contribute only slightly less than her mythology. Kaldis's punning, like his mythological references, serves to personify the landscape. Everything is alive, even the geographical symbols.

Kaldis seems to fall down only where his organization gets too casual, or where his (and Greece's) wonderful light isn't allowed its full play. *My Child Harold's Pilgrimage or Medea and the Argonauts,* 1956-1957, evidently autobiographical in some way, is strangely murky, lacking in Kaldis's habitual joy; the objects in the landscape seem somehow doomed, about to topple out of existence. And a set of six miniatures edges over towards quaintness: it's as if there isn't sufficient room in them for both the clutter and the light, or for the kind of power that the clutter acquires when presented in large scale.

Some of the paintings are organized around large areas of unpainted canvas, which are articulated here and there by dark outlines and brightly colored shapes. In the best of these, which bears the rather fancy title *White, White, A Greek Metaphysical White,* 1973-1975, the bare topography is pushed and pulled by mysterious forces, extruding a blue cape at one point and surrounded by rich blue, green, and orange sea and sky. Though they encompass many modernist concerns—several are quite abstract in feeling—the paintings resist, forcefully, attempts to pin them down. They seem rather to contain, in both subject and style, genuine life forces that

31

Kaldis, now 76, allows us to perceive without obliging us to throw off our sophistication or other predilections. Life, for a change, is rearing a sunny and pretty head.

2. Edith Schloss

Edith Schloss's modestly scaled, unabashedly lyrical, very appealing oils and watercolors combine views of the bay of La Spezia, Italy, with still-life objects from the artist's studio there. In terms of spatial organization, the combination amounts to something of a tour de force. The objects—flowers, fruit, jars, birds—are right up in the foreground, usually lined up along the bottom edge. They are painted in a flat, droll, childlike manner sometimes verging on abstraction, and often in bright, highly saturated colors. Sometimes they appear to be resting on the beach, or conceivably on a windowsill, but most often they aren't resting on anything, having somehow materialized, or been superimposed by force, over the other details of seascape. One has the feeling of looking past them only half successfully to the smaller, more gestural details in the distance: across a vacant middle ground (beach?) to the lovely bay in its various rich blues and moods, a few brushstrokes for a boat riding the waves, and finally a green lump of island with a mark indicating a lighthouse.

The paintings work in terms of the contrast, as well as the connection, between these seaside studio objects and the sea itself. There are as it were two focuses: close-up and long-shot. The presence of relatively large white areas, particularly in the most recent paintings, helps to keep the bright, decorative color from being too pretty. Whereas in some of the oils from the early '70s the luscious reds of flowers or the greens and yellows of other objects are somewhat confectionary against the blue of the sea, paintings like *Squall,* 1975, and *Last Sunday in August,* 1976, seem to have seen and solved the problem. The new paintings are somewhat tighter and calmer as well, with more defining of areas.

One of the best paintings in this show was *La Festa,* 1976, which has a flaming red sea (the only such) and which includes a bemused-looking elephant facing left and a bird facing right in a witty caravan of more and less animate things along the bottom. As one moves from painting to painting, the still-life figures become old friends, queueing up for some mission we know nothing about (unless it's just to get together to look at the sea), tall, short, elegant, frumpy, abstract, realistic, painted-in, transparent. They sometimes sprawl awkwardly, seemingly at random, looking rather lost, but always appealingly so. In their deployment and deportment, their aura of somehow belonging where they are, they convince one that this is what objects must be like, this is what they do when left to their own devices.

Schloss's roots are in the Abstract-Expressionist '40s, and it is clear throughout her work that both feeling and form come from within as well as without. The boxes she exhibited in the '50s and continues to make (though no longer considering them her major work) combine very small found objects in an understated lyricism. Restraint is a key to the success of her paintings as well. Her recent show was a mini-retrospective, including paintings from the past eight years as well as several of the boxes. Eight watercolors formed a series in themselves, more even in tone and abstract in feeling than the oils. On the whole her successes are small rather than large, which isn't to demean them; they are genuine and they come often.

Her angle is indeed fresh and always lively, her eye for contours and her placements are invariably right. With subject matter as potentially dangerous as the glorious Mediterranean, her restraint—amounting to tact—seems especially appropriate.

ABSTRACTION AND ELIZABETH BISHOP

It seems to me that the poet who chooses to stay outside the "international modernist" movement of the past 125 or so years has to be awfully good to succeed. Elizabeth Bishop is an interesting case in point. The poems she writes mostly appear in *The New Yorker*. They look conventional on the page and they employ conventional strategies, surrounding (and epiphanizing) objects, people, and situations. But though she looks to be a member of a vast and persistent Academy, she has managed to set herself far apart from poets who seem to be doing the same things.

There are many reasons for that, some of them well-documented. Her eye and ear are terrific. What she chooses to notice is invariably interesting. She has an uncanny gift for raising the conventional to the sublime, a special sublime, graceful and muscular, colloquial and tight as a drum. It is this muscularity, this toughness of both mind and language, that keeps her landscapes from either clutter or preciosity. Moreover, certain qualities that are as much a part of the poet as of the poetry come through steadily: curiosity, caring, tolerance, gentle amusement, humanity.

Two qualities which I find especially interesting, and important, in her poetry verge on abstraction—surprising in one who virtually stands for concrete particularity. The first is a homogeneous tone and movement in certain of her best poems—what in painting is

[*Poetry Project Newsletter,* July 1978]

called an "allover" surface. Although poems such as "Florida," "Cape Breton," and "Over 2000 Illustrations and a Complete Concordance" appear to develop, they don't really go anywhere. A resonant question or statement at the close, together with the general treatment of spatial details as temporal ones, gives an illusion of movement. What these poems do is make statements, relentlessly. The statements follow from one another, in general, but each is curiously discrete also, as if it were trying to establish its own identity apart from the poem. Everything looks connected ("by 'and' and 'and'") but the connections are at least as magical as rhetorical; the voice is the glue. With the building up of details, of all kinds and on all levels, phrase piling on phrase, appositive on appositive, a very special resonance occurs above and apart from the "meaning." Even those poems that have a plot also have this incremental music. When a transition comes, it's so rare and so unemphasized that the effect is quietly dazzling ("Entering the Narrows at St. Johns..."; "Thirty or more buzzards are drifting down, down, down...").

The other special, semi-abstract quality has to do with individual words. Certain fastball pitchers are said to throw a "heavy ball." It has always seemed to me that Elizabeth Bishop's words weigh more than other poets' words. Or they're lit from behind. Or they occur naturally in 20-point type but our eyes have been magically clouded. There is a presence to her language in and of itself. In part, the words refuse to be read with the eyes alone. But they also refuse to be swallowed up in their referential duties: they're physical, stubborn: they stay words. I suspect this has to do particularly with sound—with consonant strength, line breaks, cadencing. (I think she has few peers with regard to all three.) The lines break in such a way that you're forced to remember that poems are words, which may be combined to form lines, statements, images, and so forth.

There is a blockiness—almost an awkwardness, as some have felt about Wyatt as compared to Surrey—in the way sounds jam up against one another, within the lines and around the bends and breaks. And there is a clarity that shines through.

Bishop is not, of course, an abstract poet. Along with poems that evince these hard-to-pinpoint components, she has always written poems that narrowly skirt the anecdotal/conventional (/sentimental) and are transformed—at least as often as not—by dint of her sensibility. The disappointments I do have usually relate to this anecdotal strain. In her successes the resonance and the rest of the magic seem to grow naturally out of her attention to particulars, subtly and without modernist fanfare—which places her in the position, as far as I can see, of being both appreciated and under-appreciated (by those who prefer their originality sounded more loudly) for the wrong reasons.

I like her new book, *Geography III,* very much. The force operating is perhaps not as intense as in some earlier work, and a few of the jewels, e.g., the parentheses closing both "Five Flights Up" and "Night City," don't seem quite sufficient to carry their settings. As those fastball pitchers say, after losing a no-hitter in the seventh inning: What do you want? "The End of March," a lovely poem that achieves an eloquence out of all proportion to its conventional setting, and "The Moose" (whose central epiphany, perhaps perversely, I like less than the rest of the long poem) are vintage Bishop. "12 O'Clock" is a clever tour de force—but see "Rainy Season; Sub-Tropics" in her *Complete Poems!* As usual, there is the feeling that she knew exactly what she was doing, everywhere. I can't think of anyone, with the possible exception of the poet James Schuyler, who does so much with observed details. There are a handful of poets whose every poem is worth attention, and Elizabeth Bishop has been in this category for over 30 years.

WORDS FROM F. T. PRINCE

This small but extraordinary *Collected Poems* was cavalierly dismissed by the *New York Times* reviewer last spring. Attention was paid to Prince's World War II poem "Soldiers Bathing"—this would seem to be party line—but that was about it; and I suspect that the set-piece aspect of that poem rather than its inherent beauties is what is keeping it alive. (It has represented Prince in endless printings of Oscar Williams's *Immortal Poems*.) The truth is that Prince's poems, the best ones, are among the marvels of English language poetry, and that this South African-born poet, with a handful of brilliantly performed, emotionally and musically rich poems, redeems build-ingfuls of modern English verse from the arid intellectuality it is famous for.

I see Prince as the passionate historian, the passionate scholar, emphasis everywhere on passion, which sometimes breaks through the scholarly reserve but most often smolders just beneath it, with the result that the poems are charged with feeling plus the sense of a struggle to hold it back. His inspiration is largely from books. His heroes, whether speakers of dramatic monologues or subjects for meditation from the outside, are historical personages, most often exiles, from native land, from civil rights, from youth, from love. And yet upon this relatively conventional base he builds poems that are original in their voice, their music, their diction, their quality of

[*L=A=N=G=U=A=G=E*, January 1980]

feeling, and most strikingly in their baroque (mannerist?) syntax, which, without abandoning its referential obligations—indeed, which succeeds in the most subtle nuancing, playing off itself, qualifying, extending, reversing—clearly becomes a prime element for its own sake, and finally a part of the meaning of the poem in a way we have come to recognize as distinctly modern.

Prince's unquestionable masterpieces "Epistle to a Patron" and "Words from Edmund Burke" appeared in his first book, printed in 1938 when he was 26. As his poetry develops, the rhetoric for its own sake—it both is and isn't—comes to be more and more in the service of feeling, until in the major poems of the 1970s, "Memoirs in Oxford," "Drypoints of the Hasidim," "Afterword on Rupert Brooke," and "A Last Attachment," a pared down, much more transparent language is used to present feeling, almost as if Prince had made a conscious resolution to put youthful things behind him. Feeling is the key, perhaps it deserves to be called the theme, of the whole book, which closes with a virtual ode to feeling on the subject of that curious case Lawrence Sterne and his emotional excesses.

At its height, Prince's poetry is a bravura of conjunction and apposition: once a poem gets going, permitted sufficient space and freedom, phrases and clauses unroll in marvelous cadences, continue beyond any bounds of "good writing," until, at least a part of the time, conventional meaning seems to be along for the ride. Prince handles intellectual matters, of which there are many in the poems, in the manner of the Metaphysicals for whom "thought was an experience": who felt their thought. His breathtaking images and figures—"civil structures of a war-like elegance as bridges," "chambers like the recovery of a sick man" (!), "She is light and dreadful as a spear, she too leaves a gash," (!)—are as ingenious as any poet's I know, and yet they remain sensuous, tied to their bases in concrete reality. Which is to say that Prince the Milton and Shakespeare scholar is, in his best poetry, a brilliant poet. It seems to me that we feel his thought as well, just as we feel and savor his weighty, opulent language.

In general, although there are some beautiful ones, the weaker poems are the short lyrics, where too much Donne, too much Yeats, too much Verse, or too much convolution in too small a space obscures rather than presents. (If you turn the tables on language, you have to be prepared for language's fighting back.) The late poems, at least for me, remain problematic. Although I find the "Memoirs" affecting—a kind of Wordsworthian Prelude working through early difficulties and trying to make sense of them, including the decision to be a poet—it is a curious poem with its simplified language and rimed, metered stanza (taken from Shelley); it has an archaic feel. The other three late pieces, "Drypoints," "Rupert Brooke," and "A Last Attachment," represent a somewhat different genre (one might call it biographical essay in verse), and are similarly affecting and similarly problematic. One admires the craft, the deft collaging from source materials, the sensitive treatment of subjects, and the will to cut through received opinion; yet one remains—I should say, I remain—unsatisfied by them. None quite transcends its subject matter, as do the great earlier poems, to which I would add "The Old Age of Michelangelo" and "Chaka" and probably "Soldiers Bathing" as well. Prince's extraordinary gifts create extravagant expectations. Which brings up the continuing, fascinating (at least to me) issue of clarity vs. reticence. Can repression be good for the poet, as opposed to the patient? Marianne Moore's advice to be as clear as your natural reticence allows you to be is only partly helpful here. The difficulty in letting feeling out, explicit in the "Memoirs" and implicit in his exiled heroes and virtual obsession with isolation and loss, underlies the earlier poems' emotional charge. Once feeling makes it out into the open, no disguises, the scholar appears to gain the upper hand: decorum overrides passion. I can't think of a happier find, for anyone, than this poet's hitting upon the dramatic monologue with its built-in distancing and licensing, post-Browning and post-Pound. It let him produce the sinewy, sensual (actually quite sexy) poems he should be famous for.

No Other Way

In "Dec. 28, 1974," one of the poems from James Schuyler's *The Morning of the Poem,* and one of the most beautiful poems I've ever read, a "clunkhead" is quoted as saying: "Your poems have grown more open." I certainly don't want to say that. But I detect an expansiveness of mood, a willingness to let more, and more kinds of, things into print as if life itself, always highlighted in a Schuyler poem, were now accompanied by a quiet stipulation: Don't exclude. The results include more intimate detail about the self (even the landscapes now seem as much about the self as about the out-of-doors); seemingly less "poetic" distance between original notations and finished poem; less direct aiming at the sublime (though the poems hit that unfashionable target as much as any being written), and as a corollary a good bit of the unlovely, the ignoble, and the downright embarrassing; and a bonus of rich anecdote and other information about the life of this superlative poet and the people and places in his consciousness.

The perceptive critic David Kalstone, in a review a few years ago, used the metaphor "perfect pitch" to try to account for the magic Schuyler gets out of "things as they are." I'm not positive it's perfect pitch, exactly, since some awkward and boring singers have perfect pitch. But I agree that some metaphor is needed. Of all the poets now writing, I can't think of one less open to the usual critical

[*L*=*A*=*N*=*G*=*U*=*A*=*G*=*E,* June 1980]

advances, more needful of direct pointing. Schuyler's work is simply beautiful, his decisions are invariably inspired decisions, whether about words or about lines (he has, among many other things, demonstrated that "skinny" lines can be as magical and unarbitrary as lengthy ones) or about conclusions or whatever. He is the farthest thing from a theoretical poet (though his intelligence is formidable) and his marvels are subtly marvelous. Which makes it very hard to talk about his work. Invariably in trying to do justice to the beauty on the page, one is reduced to saying: Look. Look how tangible, how remarkably clear, how moving, how masterful, how original. (Anyway, try explaining the dynamics, let alone the beauty, of a line carried across not merely the carriage return but across and around the *syntax,* when the arrangements are subtly varied, absolutely right and yet seemingly spontaneous, set down in just the way they occurred, which we know can't be true—at least not all the time?) As contemporary a poet as he is, mixing the highest with the lowest, often casual to the point where one feels, oh well, another Schuyler poem—feels it at first, until the poem strikes—he is contemporary, even experimental, in ways that are easy to miss; more so in that his poems imply, clearly draw upon, the riches of the poetic past. All of which has made his critical reputation far less than it should be. One hopes that finally this will change, with the help of a new publisher, the best, Farrar, Straus. Even so, it must be added that reductive, rampaging and non-ostensive critics need not apply. Maybe a metaphor from painting—or tennis?—can be tacked onto perfect pitch to round out the picture: he makes perfect placements (Chardin), never tries to out-power (Connors). The magic is in the touch, the sheer handling.

Schuyler's language, his intimate relationship with words, is one of the chief areas of his sublety. He is as interested in language as in what his language refers to and evokes, but the spotlight is so unemphatic that all that the words do on their own can be missed. If Yeats, say, and perhaps Elizabeth Bishop as well, are "lapidary," Schuyler's musical precision has the juicy lightness and sway of stems and leaves: no less perfect but more spontaneous, more like life itself; not life talking through him (as it presumably does through certain poets) but talk—art—which is a part of life rather than something over on the other side which has given rise to speculation about imitator and imitated, ways of reconciliation, etc. So that Schuyler's poems *are* words; but in the same way that the flattest of paintings are paintings rather than simply paint, his poems are a multitude of things besides. He continually reminds one of all that poems can be and do, all that can *happen* between the start of a poem and its conclusion. Yet even the more obvious effects, such as the jokes and the sharp wit that occasionally surfaces, are never apart from the poem: they're there as parts of poems, which have to do with life, which is color, weather, growth, objects, feelings, memory, structure, gossip, intelligence, humor, language, all.

The book contains a sequence of poignant poems written at the Payne Whitney Clinic in Manhattan—in the middle of which, remarkably, the poet can (1) call himself "Jim the Jerk"; and (2) ask, as naturally as you would ask about the weather, the $64 question: "What is a / poem, anyway?" When it comes to the title poem, 60 pages long in lines many of which are long enough to be two lines, it becomes clear that Schuyler can do just about whatever he wants.

"The Morning of the Poem" is an outgrowth of his other long (so we thought) masterpieces, "The Crystal Lithium" and "Hymn to Life." The style is what might be termed his Ongoing style, and the poem is an Excursion: from Western N.Y. State to Chelsea, Manhattan; to Europe; to childhood; through the poet's major and minor concerns, moods, memories, pet peeves, love affairs, special landscapes; with epic digressions and sometimes dazzling trips of the switch. Taking up more than half a book, it is amazingly sustained. Whereas his shorter poems normally grow out of very specific settings, with the poet often literally sitting in the middle, here his memory and associations work to make past situations immediate: his entire life somehow becomes the specific setting. There is a tone of nostalgia, even wistfulness—but also a mood of acceptance which includes the regrets and the difficult times. Not philosophical or religious acceptance, he's not that kind of poet; but acceptance. This is how things are, played upon a guitar that is turquoise, or aqua, with sun-drenched frets.

In a characteristically modest way, Schuyler writes that he wants "merely to say, to see and say, things / as they are." But we can hardly take that "merely" at face value; the only way to take it, as I see it, is the way Yeats used it in "The Second Coming": absolutely. For all the pure observation and diary jottings, which are indeed central to his method as a poet, and which include plain or offhand statement (sometimes determinedly or even perversely so?) clearly not in the same league with his most inspired writing, one is hard put to find anything that doesn't work. And in the middle of hunting, one comes upon a small gem like "Footnote," or a larger one like "Song" ("The light lies layered in the leaves...."), or the haunting—for once that horrible word really applies—"Korean Mums." If this is the morning of the poem, then the forecast for the rest of the day must be glorious. Or as this quintessentially modest poet was moved to say, one and only one time (in a wonderful poem that was omitted from this book but will, I hope, be in the next): "Many / think that I am modest: / they could not be more mistaken. / I'm a great poet: no other way."

II

TREVOR WINKFIELD'S RADICAL DAFTNESS

To title one's New York show of paintings "Radical Daftness" (on the heels of one in London titled "Analytical Dottiness") would seem to invite a certain kind of attention, not to say a certain kind of viewer. *Whatever* is going on, it suggests, it's harmless. Well, it isn't. Winkfield's paintings, derived from flat, outlined comic-strip style, are indeed daft, and often very funny; but they resonate well beyond the exhibition space. Exceedingly strange characters—animal, vegetable and mineral, plus various combinations of the three—form strange vignettes, usually crammed into a very small space. The comic "frames" are dislocated and fragmented seemingly at random, so that whatever story line is suggested is simultaneously broken apart. Various images repeated from painting to painting, e.g., teeth, buttons, whistles, don't "mean" anything. To top it off, there are numerous jokes in the form of punning titles, visual puns, and echoes and parodies involving High Art.

This was Winkfield's second show in America and only his third overall, and he has clearly arrived: his handling, his subject matter, his sense of his direction show great confidence. The paintings, all

[*Art in America,* March 1981]

small, are done in Rowney acrylics on paper; the paint is meticulously and smoothly brushed (three coats) to look absolutely flat, print-like. The fragmented frames, together with the bits and pieces of images, give an additional appearance of collage—as though the paintings had begun as collage and then, by some mysterious homogenizing process, lost the variety of texture and material but kept the look. Winkfield's colors have grown brighter and are very appealing (they include an occasional, effective use of black and white or gray), and he often uses a great many of them in a single picture, such that the resolution amounts to tour de force. The obvious care and skill in both color and composition play against the wacky subject matter.

One of the best, and funniest, paintings is *Palette,* featuring two Englishmen on a train. The first is pointing to an incredible string of green gunk which has protruded like a science-fiction blob from somewhere overhead, landed in a semi-solid cone on the hat of the second (the palette??) and continued, while dripping, in loops to the other side of the compartment. The first *may* be supporting the paint to keep it from splashing; or he may be saying, "Nice palette!" to the other's sheepish but infinite delight. *Father and Son* stars a sailor who is a lobster from the neck down, and who is "guarding the memory" of his wife and kid back home while literally balancing that memory on his head in a parody of a comic idea-balloon— which is also a torn, heart-shaped hot water bottle.

Not all the paintings are this complicated, and not all are intended to be funny. Several verge on abstraction, among them the very small, very pretty *Swiss Still Life*. What gradually but firmly emerges from behind the radical and analytical daftness is the artist's knowingness and his good will, about art and about people (recalling that "daft" originally included the meanings "modest" and "gentle"). Winkfield feels for his misguided schmoes, like the men pursuing their idiotic *Cottage Industries* (e.g., sawing a giant pencil of a log while standing on one leg and wearing the first cut for a hat). The facial expressions he gets are strikingly accurate in human terms—sometimes priceless—which makes these vignettes, despite their dada-like absurdity, surprisingly moving. Surprise is ultimately a chief quality of the paintings, which begin by gently shocking and end by somehow convincing you, to your surprise, that surprise, like laughter, is only one of many valid responses to the work.

For all his comic vision, Winkfield's seriousness includes, as one proceeds from painting to painting, hints that are more unsettling than humorous: some intangible sense of danger underlying the dislocations, the bizarre behavior, and the mysteriously detached and fragmentary objects: What sort of world is this? Can it possibly be ours? But for now the comic spirit is predominant, and the hilarious and knowing look on the face of the human "palette" is the emblem of this artist.

KENNETH KOCH IN PUBLIC

When I said to F, Why do you write poems?
He said, Look at most of the poems
That have already been written!

[*"Days and Nights"*]

1.

On the surface Kenneth Koch's very early poems, such as those collected in *Poems from 1952 and 1953* (1968), seem as private as poems get. Dispensing with logic, plot, and in many cases "meaning," they rely instead on seemingly arbitrary diction, fragmented imagery, and rapid association. Almost any stanza is illustrative.

And the chorus
Of "Wear purple gloves like a sundae"
Circumstances the Afghanistan flowers
The feet under the hue of
The mid-Atlantic

[*Poems from 1952 and 1953*, p. 10]

Now it is Sunday and the leap year is over;
The Polish light is descending a mountain of lawyers

[1982]

Named cattle, the march is saved
From last Juno ontology. Can the basin reciprocate
African harmony's sleepy films? Negative
Poseidon! O chows. They chose to eat sleepy plates
Of grand opera, time's digressing natives,
In clockwork shoes, a medicine to shovel them violets
In the way good counsel cerebrates the scalding shore.

[p. 12]

One of the curious things about these poems is that they *are* in stanzas, and that unlike other "experimental" poetry, they respect conventions such as initial capitals, flush-left lines, and generally tidy arrangement. Another curious thing is the feeling one gets that they ought to mean more than they do. For all their incomprehensibility, the lines seem to break naturally. The syntax has a mysterious logic to it; the music of phrase and cadence is convincing. In addition, the poems are full of action and dialogue, making it appear that events are taking place—when in fact what is happening is impossible to tell from the shifting, unidentified voices and actors. It is almost as if a typist, not unfamiliar with poetry, were typing confidently with his hands on the wrong keys (or perhaps more to the point, using a simplified child's typewriter where each key produces a whole word—but still on the wrong keys). Altogether, one gets the sense that the framework or terms in which poetry ordinarily presents itself have been separated from their ordinary uses and significance. A series of transformations about which we are entirely in the dark appears to have taken place, such that we are left with, as it were, the right places and the wrong words.

An early, book-length poem, *When the Sun Tries to Go On,* has a round 100 stanzas, 24 lines each, of which the following is typical:

Yesterday an usual fainting pen bananas
Auto. Winter for my catching out flags not
Merry in my room! Denver! orbèd hags! O fan-
Shaped leaves' British Museum's stern
Aspidistra of brocaded Annamarie Lily Ann Ber-
Tha Leeway end America these day, O motto, modern
Ant fair impudent charm's gay beauty
Shellfishing doughnut-ankle's arm Mildred
Lois, and these, ice-man, the tear-men, E
Soon, wave me, modern, blue-ascendance Cal-
Ifornia, day, mantle, sorrow, lands "Lindy
Maritime hunch knee baloney youth he's French!" I
Nearly fell auto this museum! Lair-bins,
O comicals! Majesty, their green and suitable hogs'
Ten guitars which mother I climate
Sun grateful Marie-bannister-soup craving their blue
Deer, the men who cocoa lilac
Hips of peace January mistral hemp Detroit
Of saving lurid nits, O mouth, curseway to the south
Might-Helen, syllabic (bet-chair) gin-telephone
Louder than the earthware thinks! "Charles?
        Telephone.
Teeny, sure to send Dale a sun-dial."
Central are the token seas. Tender Labrador of bees,
Paper antonyms. O the hill picks up, that is pink.
        [*When the Sun Tries to Go On,* p. 69]

There is no apparent reason why a poem that reduces meaning to
the level of individual words should be organized into "regular"

stanzas. Nor is it clear why a poem that neither develops nor shifts significantly should continue for 100 pages. The contrast between superficial conventionality and flamboyant experiment is disorienting. What lingers is the notion that Koch's poetry exists *in reference to* more normal ways of writing, and that whatever significance it possesses has something to do with that relationship.

Thank You (1962), his first important collection, made two things clear. Koch was out to provoke, and he was interested less in any single poetic experiment than in the general principle of undercutting expectations: encouraging those expectations by the use of familiar modes, then pulling the rug out.

Central to *Thank You* are the poetic catalog (deriving from Whitman) and the poetic parody.

> These locks on doors have brought me happiness:
> The lock on the door of the sewing machine in the
>   living room
> Of a tiny hut in which I was living with a mad seam-
>   stress;
> The lock on the filling station one night when I was
>   drunk
> And had the idea of enjoying a nip of petroleum;
> The lock on the family of seals, which, when released,
>   would have bitten...
>   [*Thank You*, p. 66]

> My misunderstandings: for years I thought "muso bello"
>   meant Bell Muse," I thought it was a kind of
> Extra reward on the slotmachine of my shyness in the
>   snow when

February was only a bouncing ball before the Hospital
of the Two Sisters of the Last
Hamburger Before I Go to Sleep. I thought Axel's Castle
was a garage...

[*Thank You*, p. 77]

As with almost everything Koch writes, these catalogs play against lingering notions of decorum and poetic diction, as well as numerous other received and half-received ideas about what poetry ought and ought not to be. Among its other provocations, the latter passage pushes metaphor so far that it virtually ceases to operate in meaningful terms and becomes instead something close to pure language play.

Parodies like "Variations on a Theme By William Carlos Williams" and "The Artist" aim at definite targets. But one can also identify a parodic impulse in poems as various as "The Departure from Hydra," "Thank You," "Permanently," "Collected Poems," "Geography," "The Circus," and "On the Great Atlantic Rainway." Most often parody seems the genesis for a poem, while the rest is pure Koch invention.[1] Just how complex the parodying can become can be seen in the short poem "Permanently." Beginning by (outrageously) personifying the parts of speech as if for some modern fairy tale, the poem suddenly switches to a parody of textbook language (which is both lyrical and odd), switches back to its "story" while adding an outrageous joke, and ultimately subverts all that has preceded via a simile that transforms this seemingly heterogeneous content into a moving declaration of love. The poem plays against the conventions of love poetry, plays against itself, and flouts expectations at every turn.

54

One day the Nouns were clustered in the street.
An Adjective walked by, with her dark beauty.
The Nouns were struck, moved, changed.
The next day a Verb drove up, and created the Sentence.

Each Sentence says one thing—for example, "Although it
was a dark rainy day when the Adjective walked by,
I shall remember the pure and sweet expression on
her face until the day I perish from the green,
effective earth."
Or, "Will you please close the window, Andrew?"
Or, for example, "Thank you, the pink pot of flowers
on the window sill has changed color recently to a
light yellow, due to the heat from the boiler
factory which exists nearby."

In the springtime the Sentences and the Nouns lay
silently on the grass.
A lonely Conjunction here and there would call, "And!
But!"
But the Adjective did not emerge.

As the adjective is lost in the sentence,
So I am lost in your eyes, ears, nose, and throat—
You have enchanted me with a single kiss
Which can never be undone
Until the destruction of language.

[*Thank You,* p. 63]

The poem above all others that made Koch's motives, strategies,
and targets eminently clear was "Fresh Air," which made it clear as

well that, comic or not, Koch was in deadly earnest. Satirizing those who populated the "kingdom of dullness" of American poetry in the 1950s, who write in "stale pale skunky pentameters (the only honest English meter, gloop gloop!)," Koch hails instead

> the new poem of the twentieth century
> Which, though influenced by Mallarmé, Shelley, Byron, and Whitman,
> Plus a million other poets, is still entirely original
> [*Thank You*, p. 55]

He decries the young poets who "are bathing the library steps with their spit" and who, "worms," "wish to perfect their form."

> Is there no voice to cry out from the wind and say what it is like to be the wind,
> To be roughed up by the trees and to bring music from the scattered houses
> And the stones, and to be in such intimate relationship with the sea
> That you cannot understand it? Is there no one who feels like a pair of pants?
> [p. 56]

Beneath the poem's large supply of vitriol (which includes a Strangler to kill off bad poets) is a passionate belief in the immediate, the unconscious, the incomprehensible, and the dazzling—as opposed to the formal elegance and contrivance that filled the poetry magazines of the time. The determined exuberance, indecorousness, and sheer silliness of much of "Fresh Air" are themselves in direct opposition to the "restraint" and "mature talent" Koch blames for the dullness of American poetry.

Despite, then, the sophisticated modernism that underlies all his work, Koch's difficulty is not of the sort we commonly associate with private or "inner" poets. It is much more a matter of playing against well known poetic conventions than of lingering mystery or complexity. Essentially Koch is a public poet who wants very much to reach an audience, and to have that audience as large as possible.

2.

We have no
Gods
Of the winds!
And therefore
Must use
Science!
[*The Pleasures of Peace*, p. 29]

Whereas Pound, Williams, Stein, Olson, Riding, Ashbery (and almost any other modernist one can call to mind) threw over the conventions almost before they did anything else, Koch has done some of his best work within a framework of meter, rime, and genre. One intriguing implication is that Decorum, that Neoclassical monster, remains somehow important for Koch: so much so that it requires slaying in poem after poem. But certainly there is another side too. Koch's overflowing wit and invention are both ignited and channeled by conventions. He often performs at his best when

57

directly taking on some given, whether the hackneyed subject of young love, the constricting mold of blank verse (whatever "skunky" means, Koch's own blank verse could not be said, even by his detractors, to be either pale or skunky),[2] or a traditional mode like verse drama, with all its accrued connotations from the Elizabethans to Eliot. A Koch poem is a performance, which begins as it were by buttonholing the reader as if to say, "I've got a great idea for a poem," and goes on to demonstrate not that the idea was necessarily a great one but that the poet—at least a good portion of the time—has made it so.[3]

Koch's widely imitated method of teaching poetry writing in classrooms is an extension of his own writing. A student is shown what some great writer has accomplished in style, subject, tone, etc.—a "poetry idea"—then attempts something along the same lines. The method is something of a "science" of inspiration,[4] replacing the Muse, the empty desire to write, and even the celebrated anxiety of influence, with the encouraging notion that writers are always and properly inspired by other writers;[5] and moreover, that arbitrary rules (including "gimmicks") can stimulate the imagination as forcibly as more conventional rime, metrical, and structural patterns.

Koch's second important collection, *The Pleasures of Peace* (1969), features several virtuoso performances. "Sleeping with Women" is a catalog which plays a series of hypnotic, incantatory repetitions and permutations on the title phrase, gathering the unexpected, the random, and the humorous into a hymn to women, sleep, and sleeping with women. In an entirely different vein, "Some South American Poets" parodies poetic manifestos and compiles a fake anthology of "Argentine" poems. The tone is more gentle than cutting, and the fabricated poems, amusing as they are, are close to pure Koch.

58

My mouth, a cascade of kisses!
And, purely below me, your mouth too,
An equal cascade of remembrance, farms of bliss,
Evidence, preoccupation, evening stars
[*The Pleasures of Peace*, p. 53]

I look at you. Oceans of beer gush from the left side
    of my collar bone
And down my sides, until they form a crystal pool at my
    feet
In which children are swimming.

[p. 62]

The "poetics" Koch concocts for his imaginary poets, which "mocks the punditism of the masters" as Koch himself is in fact doing, is hardly more misguided or silly (and no less useful to its practitioners) than many such apologias. "Some South American Poets" is a resounding success; yet as with a great many Koch poems, the reader has to be in the know for the piece to work. The assumptions of a knowledgeable audience and of knowledge that is public underlie the effects of his poetry.

    The lengthy title poem in *The Pleasures of Peace* is a public poem on several levels, not the least of which is its occasion, the Vietnam War and general unrest of the 1960s (which Koch had an intimate view of at Columbia). The poem, defying all expectations concerning anti-war poetry, is a comic narrative involving competition between two poets, Koch being one, for a Peace Award. Within this narrative framework (which in fact continually digresses), it plays against notions of engaged poetry, the "serious subject," and good taste in general. Naturally, Koch wins the competition hands down.

Many of these poetic performances have a good deal to do with classic comic routines. The repetition in

> The big beer parlor was filled with barmaids and men
>   named Stuart
> Who were all trying to buy a big red pitcher of beer
>   for an artiste named Alma Stuart
> [*The Pleasures of Peace*, p. 96]

is comic, as are the endless oddball names Koch invents for the characters in his pieces, Mordecai La Schlomp, De Bruins, Rizitznikov, Giorgio Finogle (stolen, with slight alteration, from *Don Juan*), Sue Ellen Musgrove. Koch works by set-ups and like many comics doesn't bother to hide them. One frequently knows what a poem is going to be like, e.g., catalog, parody, from the opening line: the surprises are in the new comic turns, the segues and "zingers." Whether considered as premise and punch lines, or simply theme-and-variations, the technique is the announcement of a subject towards which readers can be assumed to have common feelings and expectations, followed by the—often lengthy—routine. In other words the poem is out in public, on stage; whatever was private in origin has been transformed. Virtuosity is of the essence, ideas are repeatable (comics proverbially steal jokes), anyone can do it. But of course very few really do it well, and no one does it in the same way as Koch.

3.

If his interest in satire and other conventional modes allied him—as it did Byron, one of his poetic heroes—oddly with the Augustans, Koch's didactic poems in *The Art of Love* (1975) separated him still further from the rest of the avant garde. Put most simply, he had arrived at a new, inspiring poetry idea: the comic, and occasionally not so comic, lecture. *The Art of Love,* drawing on Virgil and Ovid, has four lecture-poems. The most radical, "Some General Instructions," features instructions as it were on the loose: on all subjects, in no order, and with no guarantee of accuracy. It is, for example, reasonable if not always obvious that "Low-slung / Buildings are sometimes dangerous to walk in and / Out of." However, it is comic and unexpected that "A building should be at least one foot and a half / Above one's height, so that if one leaps / In surprise or joy or fear, one's head will not be injured." And it is exceedingly strange to hear that "Large / Persons, both male and female, are best seen out of doors." [p. 14] In sharp contrast to the genial, deadpan zaniness of "Some General Instructions," "The Art of Poetry" may be seen as Koch's resolution to the issues he raised in the satirical "Fresh Air." Rather than jokes at the expense of an Establishment, this poem is a compendium of all that Koch as writer and teacher passionately holds to. It is serious (though not without humor) and down-to-earth—as well as a performance. In still another vein, "On Beauty" transforms a subject traditionally fraught with vagueness and obfuscation into a lively meditation cum aesthetic tour.

The longest of the lectures by far, "The Art of Love" is in some ways the greatest achievement, in others the most problematic—and certainly the most indecorous. With a highly charged given which includes Ovid's *Art of Love* and 42nd Street pornography, Koch parodies, prescribes, catalogs, and plays against common feelings and expectations through 45 pages of frequently outrageous tour de force. The poem's problematic nature has to do with its explicit and implicit attitudes towards women. For all its shock value, Koch knew a fruitful subject for a Koch performance when he saw it.

One striking aspect of these didactic poems is their unusual clarity. They are in fact close to prose, as would befit public lectures. Yet it is important to note that Koch's poetry from the first has been marked by a kind of clarity within confusion. Whatever is difficult has much more to do with associative leaps and with the range and speed of the action than with genuine complexity, or subtlety, of ideas or language. Where ideas do figure, as in "The Art of Poetry," they are straightforward and accessible; that poem's freshness has to do with the rediscovery of basics, a kind of recovered common sense. Even a baffling work such as "The Interpretation of Dreams" is written in language comprehensible to a sixth-grader. The confusion is (appropriately) dream-like confusion: familiar elements impinging irrationally and surprisingly on other familiar elements. The poems (like dreams) remain theoretically comprehensible, unlike, say, certain poems by Mallarmé or Rilke, or Dickinson or Ashbery, which inform us that we are to take our pleasure and understanding in original ways having less to do with what is translatable into public terms than with what stays stubbornly private.[6]

In "Seine," Koch speaks of the "absurd simplicity" of his poem, which nonetheless "represents the truth."[7] Throughout his work, he deals in the realism of the mind in operation rather than the realism of the depicted outer world. His admiration for poets like Williams, Whitman, Apollinaire, and Mayakovsky is of a piece with his own writing. In sharp contrast to those "abstracted dried up boys" and symbol–mongers satirized in "Fresh Air," these poets are dazzling in their simplicity. Significantly, Koch's praise for a poet as complicated as Wallace Stevens focuses on the straightforward and declarative Stevens. If he makes an exception for John Ashbery, that may well have to do with the developing of Ashbery's work from origins in the same sort of dazzling simplicity.

Related to its common diction and uncomplicated syntax is the conversational quality of much of Koch's writing. Excepting the earliest cubist experiments, even where his language runs pell-mell Koch's is a speaking voice; his idiom is loose and conversational. Northrop Frye distinguishes between *epos,* or true oral epic, and *fiction,* or printed literature, the latter retaining only a theoretical relationship to the notion of speaker and audience.[8] Koch is somewhere between, but closer to the first. Rather than "overheard," the hallmark of lyric poetry in Frye's well known formulation following John Stuart Mill, Koch's poems assume an audience. (He is an excellent reader of poetry aloud, which is probably to the point.) Apart from stage directions and character tags, there is frequently little to distinguish his poems from his plays: both feature fragmented dialogue and action, instantaneous scene changes, non sequitur as the rule. The speakers in both are as likely to be animals or objects or otherwise "unsophisticated" personae as they are to be human beings.

"Farm's Thoughts," an early success, shows Koch to be master of a special sort of persona:

> I am the horse, alive and everything.
> On the merry-go-round I made you happy as anything.
> In these harvest fields they kick my body like a
>   plaything.

> I am the panther, soda fountain of the zoo;
> I will represent exoticism here on the farm with you.
>
> [*Thank You*, p. 25]

The exotic panther notwithstanding, there is nothing exotic about the lyrical, childlike language. Where a poem has no specific persona, it is often possible to recognize some voice adopted for the occasion—anything from the subhuman to the human and zany to the friendly professorial. One could go so far as to argue that everything Koch writes is enclosed in quotation marks, though often invisible ones: it is a dramatic poetry. Even the love poems, where one might expect unmediated personal feeling, keep separate the man who loves and the mind which creates. The voice apparent in

> O what a physical effect it has on me
> To dive forever into the light blue sea
> Of your acquaintance! Ah, but dearest friends,
> Like forms, are finished, as life has ends! Still,
> It is beautiful...
>
> I love you fame I love you raining sun I love you
>   cigarettes I love you love
> I love you daggers I love smiles daggers and symbolism.
>
> [*Thank You,* p. 21]

is not the voice of the poet himself, at least not the whole poet. It is, if anything, the voice of pure feeling, youthfully enthusiastic, running counter to expectation. Later poems about love and other important emotions and feelings work similarly, like the strong and moving "Alive For An Instant":

64

I have a man in my hands I have a woman in my shoes
I have a landmark decision in my reason
I have a death rattle in my nose I have summer in my
    brain water
I have dreams in my toes
This is the matter with me and the hammer of my
    mother and father
Who created me with everything
But I lack calm I lack rose

[*The Art of Love,* p. 11]

His verse epics in ottava rima, *Ko* (1959) and *The Duplications* (1977), represent Koch's crowning achievements in public poetry. Pound, Williams, and Olson wrote what we have come to consider modern epics—poems of real length and scope of a specifically contemporary nature. Koch, once more apart, begins with centuries-old epic conventions and with two well known epic poems, Ariosto's *Orlando Furioso* and Byron's *Don Juan,* and pushes "epic machinery" to comic extremes. The brilliantly rimed *Ko,* to take only one of its outrageous aspects, "out-meanwhiles" just about any other narrative in existence. *The Duplications,* coming almost twenty years later, includes sober meditation among its zany action:

The problem is, Can I pick up my story
And carry it convincingly from where
I left it trailing an uncertain glory
Through the humming, bee-filled Venice air
And plunk it down again as in a dory
In my now elder words, perhaps more bare
Of connotation and my mind less leaping
Than when I saw you last when I was sleeping

65

And saw you blossom for me every night
Just like a girl and also like a field which
Was filled with flowers, daisies yellow white
And roses pink and white, a florist's yield which
Would make him think a horrid world all right—
So were you to me.

[*The Duplications,* pp. 79-80]

As with his didactic poems, Koch transforms an unlikely idea into an immensely fecund and entirely modern one.

The epic size of *Ko* and *The Duplications* brings up one final consideration concerning the public nature of Koch's poetry. The average length of a Koch poem is well above the average. Non-epics such as "The Art of Love" and the more recent "Reflections on Morocco" grow to remarkable size. The catalog poems are theoretically endless. It would appear that Koch's poems attempt, at least implicitly, to exhaust both their subjects and whatever "poetry idea" served as impetus: his virtuosity consists partly in doing more than can "humanly" be done, in treating things somehow from all angles—a very different thing from the notion of a poet's special angle of vision. Although I would not want to push the idea too far, it seems to me that there is in Koch's work to date an ambition towards something like epic inclusiveness, i.e., taking up *all* the space, doing the thing once and for all, which, coupled with his other public aspects, is a token of shared impulses, energies, drives, and appreciation, rather than of private worlds.

The Art of Love includes one poem, "The Circus," that stands out from the rest of the book as well as from everything Koch published previously. "The Circus" presents circumstances surrounding the composition of the much earlier poem of the same name. The whole atmosphere is new for Koch.

> I remember when I wrote The Circus
> I was living in Paris, or rather we were living in
> > Paris
> Janice, Frank was alive, the Whitney Museum
> Was still on 8th Street, or was it still something else?
> Fernand Léger lived in our building
> Well it wasn't really our building it was the building
> > we lived in
> Next to a Grand Guignol troupe who made a lot of
> > noise
> So that one day I yelled through a hole in the wall
> Of our apartment I don't know why there was a hole
> > there
> Shut up!
>
> > [*The Art of Love*, p. 3]

The conversational idiom is now in the service of something close to genuine conversation; the brash confidence of *Thank You* has been replaced by middle-age uncertainties. Although the poem repeats its title phrase, it does so less as formula than as a naturally recurring association of memory and feeling. Humor is by no means excluded, but one senses a new quality of seriousness, and that these poems mean to stay with their subjects in a way that earlier poems did not. The same will to be serious shows up in his next book as well. "The Boiling Water" in fact plays off the idea of seriousness.

> Serious, all our life is serious, and we see around us
> Seriousness for other things, that touches us and seems
>   as if it might be giving clues.
> The seriousness of the house when it is being built
> And is almost completed, and then the moment when it
>   is completed.
> The seriousness of the bee when it stings. We say, He has
>   taken his life,
> Merely to sting. Why would he do that? And we feel
> We aren't concentrated enough, not pure, not deep
> As the buzzing bee.
>   [*The Burning Mystery of Anna in 1951*, p. 44]

Tone and subject are closer to Whitman here than in Koch's earlier catalogs. Though witty and far ranging, this poetry is, in the context of Koch's oeuvre, sober, as much concerned with its "content" as with tour de force. "Our Hearts," "The Simplicity of the Unknown Past," "The Language of Shadows," "The Problem of Anxiety" (which contrasts significantly with "The Interpretation of Dreams"), and "In the Morning" all show this relative sobriety.

Recent long poems in magazines, such as "With Janice" and "Days and Nights," seem in various ways to combine the new Koch and the old: loosely constructed meditation, rapid associations that make it impossible to grasp the poems in conventional ways—together with a new sense of struggle to make sense out of the poet's past and present life. Is Koch a more private poet than formerly? My own feeling is that despite the increased focus on personal experience, he is still, essentially, in the business of poetic performance.[9] One could argue that both "With Janice" and "Days and Nights" play against the Romantic/meditative genre, as well as operating within it, a characteristic Koch double procedure. The new poems, as I read them, mean to reach and affect their readers and to be heard rather than overheard. The clear colloquial diction, the appealing imagery, the non sequiturs, the (good) humor, and the virtuosity are all in evidence, as is the poet vitally concerned with poetry from both sides, its creation and its appreciation.

Notes

[1] It is interesting, for example, but not terribly illuminating to learn that "Collected Poems" was inspired by another poet's forthcoming book. Apart from poking some fun at the seriousness of book publication, Koch's poem has almost nothing to do with its origins.

[2] "The Departure from Hydra" and "The Railway Stationery" are good examples of poems that work off conventional verse. Both manage to parody the ordinary (dull) uses of blank verse and also to celebrate its possibilities.

[3] Koch's little known collaborative book with the painter Alex Katz, *Interlocking Lives* (Kulchur Press, 1970), is a kind of paradigm for his poems. Responding to a series of cartoonish line drawings by Katz, Koch constructed five different story lines/captions.

[4] The poem from which the epigraph to this section is taken is about ships and Greek gods, rather than about poetry. But it seems natural in light of Koch's writing and teaching to substitute Muse

for gods and inspiration for wind.

POEM

The thing
To do
Is organize
The sea
So boats will
Automatically float
To their destinations.
Ah, the Greeks
Thought of that!
Well, what if
They
Did? We have no
Gods
Of the winds!
And therefore
Must use
Science!

[5] Koch freely acknowledges that he "always liked to be influenced," by, among others, Apollinaire, Jacob, Eluard, Reverdy, Williams, Stevens, Ariosto, Byron. (See Mark Hillringhouse, "An Interview with Kenneth Koch," *New York Arts Journal*, #25-26, p. 17.)

[6] Certainly the early "language" poems have far more confusion than clarity; I would argue that they push meaningless-ness so far that it no longer makes sense to talk about either public or private poetry. Even so their diction is determinedly down to earth, the furthest thing from elevated.

[7] *The Pleasures of Peace*, p. 71.

[8] *Anatomy of Criticism* (Princeton U. Press, 1957), pp. 248-250.

[9] "The Burning Mystery of Anna in 1951," for example, seems as concerned with the *poetic* possiblities—the tone, the music, the "flavor"—of fragmented and confused memory as it is with the psychological.

Frances Waldman

Frances LeFevre Waldman, who died on May 15th [1982] at the age of 73, was the daughter-in-law of a poet, the mother of a poet, an accomplished writer and translator herself, and in her late years a talented actress. She edited the *Poetry Project Newsletter* from 1976 to 1978. To everything she did, from literary projects to her numerous acquaintanceships, she brought an exemplary intelligence, interest and forthrightness. She was singularly helpful to young writers starting out, or starting out in New York, and in the late 1960s her house on Macdougal Street was frequently filled with poets (as well as, it seemed, every book of poems, big press or mimeo, there ever was). When a St. Mark's workshop group was locked out of the Church, it went to Frances's. She herself traveled to an extraordinary number of gatherings involving poetry, braving dark distances on foot, even in her late years: it's hard to think of anyone who supported poetry more consistently.

Frances was a wonderfully fluid prose writer. As a matter of fact, her prose seemed so effortless that more than once a letter from her left me with the depressed feeling that I had no business writing prose. I keep wondering if maybe secretly she wrote the memoirs others kept urging her to write; with her knowledge of poetic comings and goings from St. Mark's to the 92nd Street YMHA, she would have been the perfect chronicler of the exciting poetic

---

[*Poetry Project Newsletter,* November 1982]

decade that began in New York in the mid-'60s. Of her admirable translations, two books have been published: *Amour à Mort,* poems in French by the Peruvian-born surrealist César Moro; and just this year, the stirring *Border Guards,* poems of the Greek Resistance by her celebrated father-in-law, Anghelos Sikelianos. All her dealings with literature were marked by her catholic—and sharply discriminating—taste. Somehow Frances could appreciate poetry other poets wouldn't even look at. She was also fond of distinguishing between "lightweights" and "heavyweights"; and she knew what she was talking about. In a time of disturbing poetic factionalism which is threatening to deprive poets of colleagues as well as audience, her taste and her tough-mindedness stand out more than ever as the healthiest, and perhaps the most genuine, approach to the whole, strange business of poetry.

During her tenure as *Newsletter* editor, she annoyed some readers as well as contributors with her rigorousness. I once had a 45-minute telephone argument with her over a baseball analogy I had used in a review. I was sure it was brilliant, and that Frances didn't quite get it; but she wouldn't budge and I hung up fuming. The net result was that the piece as printed was clearer than I had originally written it. Of all Frances's memorable qualities, I keep coming back to her pluck. She had so much life, so much spirit, that even when her health was failing badly, it seemed she of all people would have no truck with death.

THE N.Y. POETRY SCENE/SHORT FORM

Addressed to Paul Violi★

Why are we doing this as an interview?

What does "scene" mean?

Seriously, if scene means "where it is" and the "it" is poetry, does that mean the reading spots (projects, institutions, coffee houses, bars, clinics), bookstores that do and don't stock big- and small-press poetry, *quartiers* (Lower East Side, West Village, Upper West Side, Soho), etc.? Or does it mean something vaguer, something like the State of the Art—which could conceivably have little to do with the aforementioned venues (and could, conceivably, exist in an *ironic* relation to them, i.e., maybe those are precisely *not* where it really is).

★ "To place poetry within a current geography (for the benefit especially of British readers) a message went out appealing for an essay on 'the current New York poetry scene.' What came back was Charles North's *Short Form*, the genesis of which is best described by Paul Violi: 'North and I sat down with a tape but I could say nothing worthwhile, let alone write an essay. So Charles put it together in this format, a sort of questionnaire to me, which I left unanswered. In other words, it's all his, and besides he puts the answers in the questions.'"—Martin Stannard, editor, *Joe Soap's Canoe*, Spring-Summer 1983.

To what extent does one's perception of the scene depend on one's aesthetics? A. A great deal.

What is poetry?
(Just kidding, I know you know.)

If "scene" has something to do with health, vitality, quality, and opportunity, characterize the N.Y. Scene.

The N.Y. Scene is clearly a number of scenes, most of which have little to do with New York per se. As we all know, the "New York School" tag which everyone associated with tries to snip off (with only moderate success and properly so) has to do with a state of mind, a sense of *Europe*, and the sense that the world is mad, rather than with this oceanic city.
(Not a question.)

Name some parts of the N.Y. Scene. Which of those, e.g., "original" N.Y. School, St. Mark's, etc., have additional parts, e.g., second and third generations, splinter groups (Bolinas, Naropa), etc.?

Is it logically possible to make any meaningful generalizations about the N.Y. Scene?

How parochial is your view of things (anyone's)? For example, what do you know about the Brooklyn poets apart from the redoubtable Bob Hershon and the *Some Mag.* crowd?

Who, apart from present company, are some of the interesting N.Y. poets, keeping in mind that you can't remember all of them at any one point and are likely to offend many? Do you think in terms of "movements" or factions?

Do the large venues, the 92nd St. Y, the Guggenheim Museum, the Academy of American Poets, have anything whatsoever to do with the N.Y. Scene?

Why is there a sense that the best lack all conviction while the worst are full of polemical intensity, that things have somehow gone awry, and that N.Y.'s fabled energy is more fable, or rather more mere energy, than formerly, or is that only my sense, bound up with my own limited perspective and efforts at selfhood?
(Choose two.)

Do any of the following apply to any, few, or all of the scenes and portions of scenes described (by you, one hopes) above? World-weariness, careerism, art-world madness—speaking of which, when we tried to do this on tape and failed miserably, we did seem to agree that the current state of the art world, always in the picture for N.Y. poetry at least since the golden-haired fifties, has something to do with what's *wrong* in the poetry world, something like, the loss of "quality," the overpowering of literature by performance (notwithstanding the rightful claims of the latter), the much publicized and boring, the excellent and retiring, etc. etc. If I seem to be grinding an axe, that is because it is somehow continually being handed to us at the zenith of dullness.

What is your perception of the national perception, if such a thing can be considered, of the N.Y. Scene? (I have in mind the ridicule in varying degrees received by the N.Y. School Poets, St. Mark's, etc., over the years. Has this changed?)

Here's an interesting one. Do you think John Ashbery together with his acclaim has had a positive or negative effect on attitudes towards New York and its poetry? I can see several sides to that. What about the meteoric aspect of his ascending the poetic heavens?

There are, as I think we said on that selfsame dismal tape, loads of poets in N.Y. who aren't very different from poets elsewhere, as I think is probably the case always. The business of the "prevailing style," the common idea of aim and effect, tone and language, grants and nepotism (just kidding). Could you characterize that style and give some idea of how many poets it applies to, and what all this has to do with N.Y.?

No? Then I guess it's my own idiosyncratic and simplistic way of bringing order to chaos.

How imporant is St. Mark's city-wide? nation-wide? (*Descriptive* linguistics.)

Does big-press publishing, centered in N.Y., producing a limited number of poetry books each year which appear in most of the bookstores, having nothing to do with the N.Y. Scene—whereas, for example, Sun Press, Full Court Press, and Kulchur Press do—

How would you change the N.Y. Scene, if you had 3 wishes? (Short answer.)

Is N.Y. still the center of the universe?

The "language" "poetry" phenomenon has one foot in N.Y., which seems proper, the latter being the modern-day Babel. As a lot of us have flirted and more with that sort of writing and continue to be as interested in language as we are in the striving depicted world, would you feel it proper to comment on those of our colleagues in N.Y. who have given themselves over to language without fear?

Is "criticism" a part of the N.Y. Scene?

Is the *N.Y. Review of Books*? The *N.Y. Times Book Review*? *N.Y. Magazine*?

Is the continuation of gentrification, "sliver" buildings, condo and co-op conversion, and cynical design?

Speaking of criticism, which is a sensitive and important issue, does whatever you said above about it constitute a plea for a more informed and aware response to what's going on in some areas of poetry *now*, a profound disappointment at the missed opportunities in the widely read organs, missed opportunities for *poetry* is what I mean, its health, distribution, and ability to excite?

Do you ride the subways to work? how many taxis do you take in a month? do you believe in commuting? do you walk to poetry readings? are there too many readings in this area so that the *idea* has lost something essential? can there never be enough readings? should poets be helped to produce poetry? do you believe in poetry on the page? is it significant that Schuyler wasn't noticed nationally until well into his 50s? do you think there will be, or is there currently, an Ashbery backlash? is O'Hara likely to go down in history as a

"major" poet? does the *New Yorker* emanate secretly from Connecticut? does what poets in N.Y. do to earn $ say anything significant about the N.Y. scene? does anyone in England (presumably those who will read this) care about any of these?
(Answer in order.)

What about Third World poetry in N.Y.?

I keep having the feeling that this scene business is fundamentally elusive, essentially so, that it looks different to everyone who looks at it. It probably has to do with age as much as poetics. When you're starting and come here from the Midwest (or The New School) it's one thing, when you've sat through a thousand readings and resented a thousand bookstores for not stocking what you think is important, it's another. Let's title this Disillusionment of the Eighties. I know a lot of people don't feel this way. It's interesting, Frances [Waldman] really was someone in a position to have an overview. We should dedicate this to her. I didn't entirely go along with her taste, of course, it was somewhat over on the conventional side in spite of everything, but she was properly removed from each specific scene and somehow clearly saw it as well. This is off topic. The question is, to what extent does commenting on a poetry scene produce that scene which, until that point, didn't quite exist?

Is this too long already?

Let's return to the art world/poetry world connection. I assume everyone gives lip service to that. Name some real ways in which the N.Y poetry scene is as it is because of the way the N.Y art scene is (not necessarily direct influence, such as, though it's certainly true for some, having painters for friends and lovers causes one to see things in other ways, try to do similar things with words—though *not* to paint with them). Jimmy (S.) titled his short prose piece in the poetics section of the Allen anthology "Poet and Painter Overture"; Ashbery's the art critic and writer of master-pieces such as "Self-Portrait in a Convex Mirror"; O'Hara wrote, curated, mentioned, hung out with, adored; Koch was and is extremely close to; Edwin Denby and Barbara Guest similarly. And among our "younger" poets, Berrigan, Padgett, Ratcliff, Schjeldahl, Yau, Yourgrau, Berkson, Towle, Shapiro, Lauterbach, Welish, Green-wald, me, you, and others. Writers have married painters, gone on vacations with them, enjoyed a cool glass of beer on a sweltering day in front of the N.Y. traffic while talking about everything under the poetic sun. John Yau was and for all I know still is a house painter. So in one sense, one (rather large it's true) group keeps alive the poetry/painting connection. Oops, forgot the other way around too, Rivers, Katz, Motherwell, Dine, Freilicher, Winkfield, Bluhm, Guston, Dash, Schneeman, Jacquette, Paula North, Jean Holabird, etc. etc. What about other groups? This isn't what I mean. I mean what Schuyler was, essentially, talking about: the air we breathe. I see it for better and for worse, worse meaning, these days if not before, the Business of art, the business of the meteoric, as well as those other problems tossed off above; *better* meaning the desire of every poet to do something as beautiful as some of the paintings we see around us every day. And the sense that art is important, part of the scheme of things, easy, or easier, for painters to feel nowadays—the actual importance, if any, of Schnabel, Salle, et al being a whole other issue—than for poets to feel. Or is that a wild understate-ment. So Art, art acts as a kind of emotional resource, the business management side of the Muse, as well as whatever it performs in the way of specific and general cross–influences, inspirations, and the like. What was the question?

Would you like to reject those questions you feel are too frivolous? Does frivolity have something essential to do with the N.Y. Scene?

For, we know that some poets from more rural, or less frenzied, areas of the country think that N.Y. poets (by which they mean, more or less, the amplified N.Y. School) are, by virtue of being in the grip of the "artificial and curtailed life," subject to a decadence that forces them to the peripheries of life, poetry and the American Way. Don't we?

Why, by the way, isn't music, N.Y. being a world–class concert hall, more important to the N.Y. poetry scene than it is? Or is it? Consider jazz, rock, punk, Cage, Thompson, poet/instrumentalists, aspirations towards the condition of music, the poetic equivalent of Muzak, the Drones, hymns to intellectual beauty.

I'm running out of gas, in case you haven't noticed. Time to end, or go to your questions, or get my typewriter, the manual, fixed. It broke after page 1 of this, and I see now that the questions got less coherent after I switched to the electric portable, some sort of comment on technology, which brings up a slew of further considerations regarding the influence of environment upon city attitudes, like winter sunlight on an otherwise disengaged scene.

What about "subject matter"?

Be sure to reread your answers.

Forty Years Later:
The Poems of David Schubert

David Schubert is a remarkable poet who died in 1946 at the age of 32 in a mental hospital on Long Island, following a life devoted to poetry, poverty, and self-destruction. He had some success in his lifetime but not much; today his name is hardly known. This special edition of *Quarterly Review [David Schubert/Works And Days]* attempts to set matters straight. It gathers the poems from Schubert's only collection, the posthumous and long out-of-print *Initial A*, together with appreciations, early work, letters, and memoirs, the last three collaged with bits and pieces of contemporary news, literary politics, and personality theory to form a "Multi/Auto/Biography."

Schubert has always struck me as being in a class by himself. Although his poems sometimes recall Hart Crane's, particularly their indirect, allusive way of presenting experience, no other poems I'm aware of have the same flavor, the extraordinary mix of complication plus sheer human pathos. Rarely does a Schubert poem make it through to the end without interrupting itself several times, or entering involved parentheses, or taking any number of surprising and apparently unwarranted turns. And yet few poets can be so touching and resonant.

[*American Book Review*, July–August 1985]

I reached a point where there was no
Use going on: my companion said, "Do not waken
The watchman, do not shout, he will die
Of shock if you make the slightest
Sound." I stood in the utter darkness,
Cold. Without evidence of myself.

The technique of diversion con-
Founds the rival by simulating friendship or
As the Victorians might say, worming
Affections. Then, at the point of trust,
As on this dark stage where one man sleeps
Slumped by the flashlight, to change the
Mode of address, from friend-
Ship to a complete stranger, to shriek-
Ing subtlety, to innuendo, and back to
Friendship. The executive wishes to
Demoralize his employee, perhaps he is slightly
Jealous?

I do not know. At the time I could not enjoy
The enchanting silly coffee waves, sometimes
Sapphire, which is the fluid stream of our life.
Since then, like William James, I have learned
Ice-skating in my August, after—

At that point I returned;
Since there was no point going on I went back,
I spoke again to the marvelous friends of
My youth: for a short while it was a life.

That you were not willing I am sorry.
["Another Poet Called David"]

As hard as it is to pin Schubert down, his mature poems fall somewhere between pure lyric on the one hand and, on the other, meditation of a highly unusual, discontinuous sort. He is always trying to make sense of experience, past and present, which threatens mightily to defeat him. Tender- and tough-minded by turns, the speaker at the heart of the poems is vulnerable in the most literal sense, haunted by childhood (which in Schubert's case was genuinely tragic), often about to be swept under; yet somehow able via wit and pluck to pull himself out—and to keep an *un*confessional distance between poet and poem. Nor does his recurring anguish preclude verve, humor, moments of joy, or charm. It is striking how many of the poems, seemingly mired in the intricacies of his despair, manage to turn upwards at the very finish, pointing ahead optimistically, if sometimes desperately so, to new beginnings. The sense of beginnings is strong throughout his work, in his abrupt, self-contained stanzas and bumpy line connections as much as in the sudden switches in tone, language, feeling, and thought that are the rule rather than exceptions. As for the literal beginnings of his poems, they are most often ingenious, and sometimes startlingly original.

All of which is to say, Schubert's poetry is fascinating and by no means easy to follow. I find him, in his best poems, reminiscent of a clever boxer, who rather than singlemindedly stalking an opponent, circles, jabs, and, as they say, gets back out, intuitively knowing when to improvise and when to go by the book. For all his knowledge of the craft, there is no irritable reaching after fact and reason—or knockouts. Instead, he is himself, allowing the feisty, pugnacious side of his sensibility equal play with the sentimental. The poems thus proceed as they do, in quiet and loud, unsettling and sometimes dazzling fashion, through their convolutions and stops, unified by the vital concerns and the unique voice speaking them.

Among many strengths, one that stands out is his mastery of the conversational enjambed line, gently muscling the reader from margin to margin. I like very much the statement Schubert wrote to accompany his selection of poems in *Five Young American Poets* (New Directions, 1941), which includes the following sentence: "Naturally, they are one: meanings and music, metaphor and thought." I especially like the "naturally." Whereas the complexities of his poetry can seem merely contrary at first glance, their complication is an integral part of a unique sensibility.

It seems ungrateful to complain even a little about such a laudable and important (if still secretly so) project. But I don't go much for the "Multi/Auto/Biography" collage that takes up two-thirds of *Works and Days*. I sympathize with the desire to put this extremely moving poetry in context. However it looks too often as though the poems are playing second fiddle to the life. At the very least, the treatment seems, ironically, premature. There is also a Public Television ring to the ghostly edifying voices that enter on the heels of poignant poem fragments. Not that the information isn't moving to one who already cares about the work, but that the atmosphere is too familiar from media attempts to bring Art to the People. Maybe I'm being proprietary, Schubert has that effect, but I kept wishing for more conventional biography.

Certainly the splendid thing, aside from the editors' devotion, is the reprinting of *Initial A,* which seems to me one of the most beautiful books of poetry this country has produced. Judging from the excellent set of appreciations (Horace Gregory, Irvin Ehrenpreiss, John Ashbery, and James Wright, among others), Schubert brings out the best in readers, and one hopes that this select group will grow to its proper size.

STATEMENT FOR OUT OF THIS WORLD

The Poetry Project has meant a great deal to me. The first poems I published, hesitantly, were in *The World* (1968), the first reading I gave was there in 1970, and the first publisher I had was Larry Fagin's Adventures in Poetry. I was also encouraged tremendously by sitting in for a couple of months on a workshop given by Tony Towle in 1970, without which, who knows. And, especially in the beginning, I went to every Wednesday night reading, or almost. So that whatever sensibility I was forming when I began in the late '60s was certainly helped along by reading, hearing, and meeting a large group of other young poets who had gravitated in some fashion to St. Mark's (in many cases from Columbia or The New School). This isn't to minimize the differences I have had with prevailing styles and attitudes there (as Frank O'Hara said of something else, "a useful thorn to have in one's side"), nor my own private share in the disgruntlements, disenchantments, and entropies that have been part of the St. Mark's aura for 20 years. Nor have I, despite all the readings, collatings, and magazines, teaching a workshop and serving on the Advisory Board, lost the feeling of being a visitor (maybe partly because it takes me 40 minutes to get there by subway). But really, there's no other *center* as far as I'm concerned. Where else do you go to hear those who inspire you? What other reading every two

[1986; printed in *Out of This World,* edited by Anne Waldman (Crown, 1991)]

which it moves (often but not always New York City streets) are sweeping statements sometimes of a quasi-philosophical nature. A female figure can be a lover, a Muse, someone hanging out on the street, or a sheer indescribable:

> She came as a falling star to the lakes. She the lithesome virgin not to be turned into a tree, she who would never dress like a penguin. An original want-not, she believed in philosophy, but she called it faith. And so her talk entered my lungs and came out as a call to the innumerable vessels that are the wives of time.
>
> ["My Mother, Life"]

I don't know about you, but that's the way I prefer my hymns to intellectual beauty.

Did I say elegant? "Wounded, sainted, and unchaste. And that was only my hostess." It's tempting to consider Godfrey a poet's poet in the best sense—but only if you consider Groucho Marx a comedian's comedian. Godfrey concocts poems which are distinctly American for all their knowledge of other poetries, and which speed along as a certain kind of poetry has sped along in America since, say, the early '50s, Godfrey's own idiom being a paratactic jazz (neo-neo-bop?) with nothing cool about it, a kind of elegant staccato. All the same, there's not much that won't stand up to close inspection. Not that every remark is meaningful, or even "meaningful"; but as far as the poem is concerned it doesn't matter. Statements whizz by together with images in a narrative that clearly makes sense to the poet, who keeps convincing the reader that that's the only requirement.

The freshest thing perhaps about the whole enterprise is that here genuine invention, intellect, humor, feeling, love of language are transformed into poetry—and it is even in prose, as Frank O'Hara would say—which doesn't turn around and betray any of them. Say, François Villon, Groucho Marx and the Englightenment *philosophes* having a series of chance encounters (as Rosemary Clooney and Alban Berg would appear to be doing in one of the pieces). Which isn't to say that Godfrey hasn't read Hart Crane and Baudelaire too, or for that matter Allen Ginsberg, Jim Brodey, and Raymond Chandler. And he's listened to a lot of jazz.

To *The New York Review of Books*
(Unpublished)

This is occasioned by Helen Vendler's positive review of James Schuyler's *Selected Poems* (*NYR*, September 29, 1988), towards which anyone in his right mind, at least anyone who cares about modern poetry, ought to feel gratitude. The review accounts for some of Schuyler's aesthetic waywardness, his position apart, not only from well known mainstreams historical and contemporary, but also from those New York School poets with whom he is often associated. It places him in a context of important forerunners, Hopkins, Whitman, Stein, Stevens, to name a few. And it takes Schuyler's life's work seriously, as few critics have done, and makes useful points about his embracing of the banal and homespun along with the extraordinary. I respect Helen Vendler and her continuing efforts to come to terms with those who are writing at the same time she is, by no means an easy task in the post-modern world, if it ever was. What leaves me uneasy is her approach.

Early on, Vendler states that Schuyler "has increasingly refused to write a 'well-made poem.'" Later she quotes Schuyler's very early (and only, so far as I know) villanelle and compares it with his late work. The villanelle's title is "Poem"—"a title poets invoke when what they have written seems to them to touch some rock-bottom sense of their own poetics." In her introductory paragraph she

___

[1988]

remarks that "any commentator on Schuyler must first deal with the strange long poems that are scattered through his work." Let's stop a minute. Are there many good poets nowadays who *don't* refuse to write the well-made poem? Are there any poets whose poems are better *made* than Schuyler's? Villanelles and Schuyler—James Schuyler? Is that really why poets title poems "Poem?" (And if not, as happens to be the case frequently, can it form the basis for a central argument, as in this review?) Must a commentator begin with the long poems when, for many devotees of Schuyler's work, it is the short lyric poems that are the quintessential Schuyler, at the very least equally important—unless starting big is a way to convince, and be convinced, that one's critical efforts are justified, serious matter for serious attention. And the epithet "strange," so casually added. What sort of literary context, or literary consciousness, must one frequent in order to find Schuyler's wonderful poems strange? What does that innocent-sounding word say about the conventional critical framework?

I want to keep this brief, and friendly, but the following remark midway in the review belongs here:

> To a reader enamored of reticence, intellectual phrasing, complex structures, or conspicuous ornament, Schuyler's talky linear [linear?], patchy pastoral daybooks...can seem diffuse and unsatisfying. To the admirer of Whitman, on the other hand, Schuyler can seem Whitman's legitimate heir (though without Whitman's astonishing imaginative flights...

Briefly, let me suggest that the two alternatives are hardly either/or; and moreover, that although Whitman's imaginative flights can be used to hit any poet over the head, Schuyler has astonishing flights of his own. Schuyler and Hopkins? Schuyler and Stevens? Schuyler and Gertrude Stein? Schuyler and the villanelle? Granting some truth to these associations, does the compulsion to "place," historicize, touch critical bases outweigh the responsibility to come to terms with *this* poet? Towards the close of the piece comes the statement, "I have read him for years with the partial incomprehension of one less alive to visual effects than he, and one less willing to investigate the aleatory." That's quite an admission, partly admirable to be sure. However, I feel bound to say (1) that the critic's "willingness" or not doesn't seem to me the issue; (2) that in Schuyler's case it is the *immediate* rather than the aleatory which is at the core, as it is in a lot of modern poetry; and (3) that it's hard to see how visual effects can be played down without doing serious harm to the critical enterprise.

Ironically, Vendler is one of the few intelligent and knowledgeable writers to tackle the difficult business of contemporary poetry without using up that poetry as part of the program. Here she is praising an importantly under-praised poet. All of which conspires to keep the critical preconceptions undercover. In reacting, it's hard not to seem ungrateful or proprietary or both. But I find the problem, at least insofar as this review represents widespread critical habits, insidious—not simply a question of the review of Schuyler someone else would write vs. the one at hand, but the basic issue of how poetry is to be approached.

Certainly let's set down a poet's connections to the world and to other poetry; but must we ride the same horses time and again, as if the unspoken principle were that to plunge a poet into an American Mainstream, with familiar American landmarks dotting the shore (in or counter-to the mainstream, it amounts to the same thing), is to proclaim the writer worth attention—while leaving out all, or a good deal of it, that really makes him worth attention. Schuyler has written some of the most beautiful poems in the last 30 years, including poems that fit on half a page, and it's hard to imagine a reader gaining a sense of that from this review. He's also, as Vendler points out, chatty, sometimes precious, sometimes diffuse—as Stevens, an American touchstone (and what happened to the New York School and its *European* antecedents?), can go on forever, fall in love with his own pentameters, and still be a great poet.

Speaking of the New York poets, Vendler separates Schuyler from the rest at the outset: he shares only "superficial resemblances of form (short lines like O'Hara's, long lines like Koch's)." He "is not radically allegorical, like Ashbery, but literal; he is not a social poet, like O'Hara, but a poet of loneliness; he is not comical and narrative, like Koch, but wistful and atmospheric." Granting the need for summary and corner-cutting in a review, I can't see that these sweeping categorizations, however well-intentioned, help us very much. Is it conceivable that the linking of Schuyler to O'Hara and Koch was ever a matter of the length of their lines? Are Schuyler's brilliant early and middle poems wistful? Are they poems of loneliness? Can it possibly suffice to dub O'Hara a social poet, for all his social life? I would suggest that the matter of the New York School, if it's to be raised at all, is far more complex than the easy generalizing can indicate.

Themes, influences, and country of origin aside, isn't there a basic responsibility to indicate to readers—most of whom don't pay attention to poetry *because* of the way it's presented in the only places they meet up with it, or, as an ironic corollary, find the reviews more gratifying than the poetry because they surely deal in ideas—why some of it is so beautiful or moving or striking: in short, how it works, and why American poetry would be so much more barren if certain poems hadn't been written? "It is Schuyler's long and honest investigation of how natural species speak to him, and in what human settings, that makes his work worth attention." I agree, in part. If the poetry, short and long, weren't so stunning and well made in the best sense, that attention wouldn't count for much. Nor would those who find Schuyler's work a pinnacle of American poetry read it over and over.

SPLURGE II

I can't think of anyone who is writing better poems right now than Paul Violi. Many of the inspired modes, and moods, that appeared in his last book, *Splurge,* make new appearances in *Likewise:* the satirical and purely comic (including the comic "found"), the outrageous word play, the narratives and dramatic monologues, the bleak states of mind, the pure lyrics. Violi doesn't hold back. In addition, the new book has a group of terrific adaptations from the Italian, plus two long poems either of which could justify a book by itself.

A part of Violi's splurging is to be generous with words: he's an includer rather than a whittler. The somehow unwarranted and excessive—gratuitous puns, satirical cracks, unexpected surreal bits—spill out of his lines as if he can't help himself. But he can. If you read the poems fast, as if they were meant to be read that way, you can miss any number of carefully attended-to phrasings, images, and figures, many of them extraordinary; and in addition a good deal of substance. Violi is one of the few genuinely funny poets around, not merely witty, *funny.* But he's also a surprisingly careful writer.

If it weren't such a literary tag, one might consider calling Violi a Metaphysical. If anything sets his poems apart, it is the yoking together of the totally dissimilar: "Slow Lightning," "squat elegance," "champagne in a dirty glass," "a pile of junk and generosity," "absur-

[*Poetry Project Newsletter,* Summer 1988]

dity and squalor," "flowering contradiction." In all sorts of ways—oxymoron and zeugma, comic poems counterpointing more "serious" ones, inventive two-term names—*contradictions that flower* seem to be at the heart of his poetic impulse. In "Little Testament," the book's wonderful big closing poem, the speaker says what instigated the poem was seeing a "lump of gold in the road," which turned out to be "bees / who like ferocious translators / had taken on the shape / of what they were devouring: a dead frog." What an amazing, complex image. The most striking poetic mood in this book as in all his books, somewhere between disaffection and limbo, almost always contains the seeds of its own banishment, which is one reason even the "dark" poems never seem cynical or truly depressed. Another reason is the verve with which he writes. Unlike most funny poets, Violi writes beautiful lyrics too. He also undercuts his own occasionally elevated tone with phrases and quick turns of feeling that are so low-down as to seem perverse. I could go on. Among many subsets of this double-sidedness is a wonderful way he has of bringing abstractions to life and definition, often in that most literary of figures, personification: "the little wings of an immensity" (well, let's call that one "avification"), "all futility and quacking isolation" (hmm...)

> Or, as Clarity said to me,
> "Let's shoot the breeze."
>
> ["Parkway"]

Because of all the obvious humor in his work, I feel the bleaker side, apparent in the adaptations (from Cecco Angioleri, Michelangelo, Leopardi, Fra Mauro) as well as in poems in his own voice, deserves attention. There are a surprising number of references, often ironic, to emptiness, confusion, disappointment, futility. In the middle of "In Praise of Idleness," the speaker, atop a "flunkgirder" on an unfinished building—a ruin—has this ironic little talk with himself:

> Want a cigarette? Nope.
> Got a match? Nope.
> See any alternative to solipsism? Nope.
> Hedonism? Nope. Sloppy stoicism? Nope.
> Did you know that Maryland
> has no natural but only man-made lakes? Nope.

Just when it seems there is no way out of his idle, disaffected state, the "creatures of idleness," some of whom are "big and clumsy and sly / and like to lick my watch," appear, and soon afterwards the last flake of snow

> grows larger
> as it descends, and presents
> when it lands in a burst of brilliance
> the floorplan for a new building
> where every wet, beaded window
> is a picture of pleasure and expectation.
> The drops ripen, moments in the light,
> questions that, answered by a feeling,
> slide away as clear as my being,
> a drop at a time down the glass.
> When the wind blows this hard
> it's about to say something at last.
> The earth down to its bare magic,
> wind and glass, water and light.

Although he is drawn to Michelangelo's self-disgust (and his adaptation is a lively litany of complaints) and Cecco's sardonic invective

> If I were fire, I'd burn the world away;
> If I were wind, I'd blow it down;
> If I were water, I'd let it drown;
> If I were God, I'd deep-six it today.
>
> ["Sonnet"]

the Leopardi "L'Infinito" is closer to Violi's "peculiar sense of nothing," his attempts to carve some meaningful shape and gratifications out of the randomness and almost existential idleness he finds himself held by. Somehow beauty, and more specifically poetry, have a redeeming part to play. Nor is his vision of confusion anything but clear-sighted, as in the perfect couplet that closes the book:

> It is my own gift of darkness,
> less than I mean, all I can say.

The lovely "Triolet" that forms a coda to "In Praise of Idleness" (and proves that this form is not in fact impossible) seems an emblem for the plight and the hope, both.

I haven't done much, I realize, to suggest the abundant imagination at work throughout Violi's poems. Imagination, whatever it means in these rather dry, post-modern ergo propter lingua days, isn't much looked to for any light it can shed on the value of particular poems, or for that matter on poetry in general. Indeed, it appears as though poets have been "freed" to get on with their task—which seems, curiously, to strive to be anything but poets. "King Nasty" is a brilliant piece of dramatic monologue that goes on for 13 pages satirizing Hollywood and the Reign of Terror following the French Revolution. (Can the Reign of Terror be satirized? If it leaps "Out of the Pol Pot and into the frying pan," and includes heads that roll but also bounce and speak, probably so.) The reader is left not quite knowing how to respond, although fascinated horror, or else horrible fascination, seems in order. Equally imaginative in a different vein is "Little Testament," roughly after Villon, which collates a big range of real and imaginary experience, bestowing "gifts" on the deserving and undeserving, including the poet, the "occasional Nihilist."

Some shorter poems that stand out are the lovely nocturne "Slow Lightning," the absolutely hilarious "Fable: Kid Blanco" and "Drastic Measures" (each containing some real-life domestic drama just beneath the surface), and the perfect opening poem, "Abundance," which takes off from Williams' rollicking "The Dance," but the way a plane takes off from a runway: the rest of the flight is all Violi. Apparently out to depict the vibrant life of Canal Street in lower Manhattan (as Williams celebrates Breughel's depiction of a peasant fair—this is getting Platonic), the poem begins, outrageously,

> In Breughel's great picture "Canal Street,"
> restaurant customers order roast swan
> instead of chicken, hurled salad
> instead of tossed salad

—goes on to satirize a street peddler and his audience, shifts in midflight to "silver towns and sea and fields" and farmers who throw "animals, large animals, / into the air to be carried away / on the winds of exuberance"—and eventually, but only eventually, returns to Canal Street. Often the effect of Violi's exuberance is to set poems to bursting, not simply as here via random or surreal connections, but often via stretching or undercutting of the familiar ways, including formal ones, poetry operates. A portion at least of the invention and the pleasure occurs in the space between unstated poetic conventions and rule-smashing.

One potential issue I see in these poems is the rearing up of violence, even cruelty, as comic material, as background, or in some instances as the focus. It's at its most obvious in "King Nasty," which has the framework of satire for justification, but makes an appearance in a number of places, even a gratuitous cameo one (which I guess is the joke) in the title of an otherwise very pretty poem, "When to Slap a Woman." In similar fashion a few horrifying historical anecdotes crop up out of Violi's reading, one startling one involving images of faces left in ice following the siege of Leningrad, another involving the German pirate Stoertebaker who managed to run past 14 of his crew *after* he was beheaded. Well, we do live in the Age of Blue Velvet. Myself, I think much of this material (let me not fail to mention an ironic "Totem Pole" consisting mostly of beheaded figures from history), which gives a distinct edge to his writing, belongs with the "occasional nihilist" side of Violi's poetic impulse. He's not just kidding around, and he doesn't hold back. What he does do is turn whatever provides the impulse into poems which give evidence of his curiosity and learning, feelings, wit, and struggle to come to terms with private demons. He is, when the occasion arises, as tough on himself as on anyone, and he displays a sharp eye for beauty in and out of language, in and on whatever terms it presents itself.

Although a few of the poems in *Likewise,* good by most standards, aren't quite up to the book's high standard, in just about all of them Violi manages to bring off something extraordinary. Take "Private Jokes," a poem in a minor mood, which closes with a stunning image of Tragedy and Comedy as Siamese twins

> starting the day
> > in their usual way,
> washing each other's hands,
> > combing each other's hair.

Or take "Midnight Shift," which begins in a familiar mood, a limbo seemingly without means of escape:

> —But then to feel your hand instead, palm up
> on the bed like a little boat in the dark,

> with everything calm for an instant
> before out of nowhere all of you lands
> on me with a great laugh, a splash of hair.

That's singing at heaven's gate. *Not* the movie.

III

NEW YORK SCHOOLS

When Ed Friedman asked if I would participate in this panel discussion (while bending my good arm), he suggested that I concentrate on New York School poetry influences good and bad—which of course immediately brings up all the assumptions: that there is a New York School of poets (as opposed to, and in light or shadow of, the New York School of painters); that, granted its one-time existence, it continues to exist; that it's appropriate to talk about it while it exists; that so-called practitioners, as opposed to critics and historians, are legitimate engagers in such talk (and vice versa); that it's more meaningful to group poets into a school than not to do so; that *school* is a useful term for a group, cohesive or not, that is fundamentally anti-academic, etc.

To complicate matters, as if they need further complication, influence is such a fundamentally tricky business, complete with its own private anxieties, rewards, mannerisms, splinter groups, family trees, Wittgenstein families, extension schools, extended families, hyper-extension, and more. There are direct influences, one writer overtly taking over strategies, tones, subjects, even the very notion

[Presented at The Poetry Project Annual Symposium, May 1988]

of a poem from another writer (or not writing "in the manner of" but nonetheless clearly in direct lineage from); general influences, as when ideas are in the air, or filter down, or become the air itself; plus a great many types and shades of influence between.

When I introduced Joe Ceravolo, David Shapiro, and Frank Lima, all legitimate Alleged New York Schoolers, at a Museum of Modern Art reading about ten years ago, I said, "They have all been associated with the so-called New York School, which as everybody knows isn't a school at all—but which is anyway, sharing a number of things which don't become clear until you leave New York or its influence." It's no longer clear whether you can leave New York, at least poetically.

Not that the school idea isn't always useful on the critical/historical side. But the critical/historical side is never the whole story. Often, as we know, it's trumped up, which never seems to bother enough people. Or if it does, the complaints are far too often entered "for the record." So whom you ask, and whom you trust, remain essential parts of the topic.

In addition, I find myself continuing to think about the differences between schools of poets and schools of painters. The latter seem so much more a part of things. Or is that, in this case, because the New York painters represent "the triumph of American painting" (in Irving Sandler's phrase) whereas American poetry had at least one and probably several triumphs before the New York poets got started? (How many triumphs can one city have anyway, particularly when its artistic logo has been a large red flag to the rest of the country, only recently carved into an apple?) Would anyone use the word triumph about the achievements of John Ashbery, Frank O'Hara, Kenneth Koch, Jimmy Schuyler, Barbara Guest, and Edwin Denby? The answer of course is yes; but as usual the qualifiers "secret" and "secretly" would need to be added. After a certain point the qualifier gets to be the story.

I wonder too, speaking of influence, if it's possible objectively and usefully to contrast the way the New York poets have been perceived, and not only by critics, with the way, for example, the leading Beat and Black Mountain poets have become icons in contemporary American writing. Let's not even begin to speak about the Others who have raised the notion of false reputation to an art form. I would go out on a small limb and suggest that even among the Tribe of John those who have real use, in addition, for Kenneth in particular, but even for Jimmy, Barbara, and Edwin, are in the minority.

As if the New York poets, together and apart, do not represent as much of a recent triumph for American poetry as any of these others. Take one last look at what passed for poetry around about the forties and early fifties, notable exceptions notwithstanding. As vital as *Howl* remains to American writing, I would argue that "Fresh Air," "Europe," "The Skaters," *Lunch Poems,* and *Freely Espousing* are also vital. Nor would I concede that Ashbery, Koch, O'Hara and Guest are any less American for bringing some of the best influences from abroad to our earnest magazines.

★ ★ ★

General influences first. It seems to me that the New York sensibility or aesthetic has by this point filtered down, around and through much of what is being done in the name of American poetry today. (What I probably mean is much of the best of what is being done today, which is begging the question but true anyway.) And of course the influence is mostly secret. The Poetry Society certainly isn't in on it, nor are the amalgamated MFAs or the Union of University Presses.—Then how come, appearances and awards to the contrary, the state of American poetry isn't in fact very healthy?

Let's skip that one for now, though I have a feeling *it*, and none of the rest, is the real topic. Influences were so much less confusing when the second generation began to come into its own (as is probably always the case). I remember in the mid-to-late sixties how many poets around the Poetry Project, a partly owned subsidiary of the New York School (if it existed), were influenced by *The Tennis Court Oath* and *Rivers and Mountains*. O'Hara, too, was such an inspiration, even before most poets knew how much he had written and how variously. Koch had taught, literally, a lot of the writers who gravitated to St. Mark's; his sense of the enormous possibilities in poetry (akin to those discernible then in modern painting and modern European poetry, but not, surely, in Hall/Pack/Simpson et al), the pleasure and excitement in making and reading it, was infectious. Schuyler, Guest and Denby (Harry Mathews and Kenward Elmslie too), if not quite so overwhelmingly, stood as models against the horrible stuff in the leading poetry publications. Of course Ginsberg, Kerouac, Creeley, Snyder, Whelan, Wieners and others did too. I remember Ashbery, among others, denying the school idea, but it was certainly more meaningful then, in terms of pure geography, poetic heroes and enemies, lineage, small press publications, and possibilities.

So what about *now*, following the scattering of a once apparently cohesive group and the transmission—and inevitable generational tangles, transformations, ramifications, focusings and thinnings-out—of the influences via the enthusiasms of Berrigan, Berkson, Mayer, Padgett, Waldman, and all the rest of the large second generation who taught workshops from the Project to Timbuktu; and

106

following this generation's sharp turn into middle age, with additional generations, at the very least a third, teaching and writing at its heels? Does it make sense to talk about a New York School of *poets*—or a New York *School* of poets—now?

My current feeling is yes, but no. Or rather, it's not for us to say, but whatever we say is probably important (if any of this is) and will be used against us. I like to think, for example, that poetic schools can be defined by their abiding poetic heroes, but that's probably too insubstantial. Curiously, some New York poets seemingly in direct lineage from first generation New York Schoolers don't seem part of the New York School. I'm thinking of some of those who continue to write like, let's call it late Ashbery (though judging from his continuing performance it's much more likely to wind up as middle). The "language" writers, at least those with roots in New York, are at least as problematic, with their mixed influences that include the Poetry Project (which is to say, mostly second generation, most strikingly Clark Coolidge) but a variety of European and other American (e.g., Zukovsky) rhizomes as well. Herein the notion of Extension School of poets, and even hyper-extension, depending on your point of view.

As virtuosos of very different kinds, Koch is inimitable, Schuyler is inimitable, Denby is inimitable, and Elmslie is inimitable too. Ashbery is quintessentially inimitable. So why are so many imitating him? Well, for one thing he's a brilliant poet who keeps on finding new ways to be brilliant. But I would go a little further out on my limb and argue that, by and large, this round of mannerism has been unfortunate. I continue to be intrigued by the contrast between the current locus of Ashbery interest as opposed, say, to the work up to and including *Self-Portrait in a Convex Mirror.* It does seem significant that the recent acolytes—in contrast to those second generation New York poets who, initially bowled over, moved on to their own voices—came upon his work rather late, just about the time the Frenchifying of the American mind via the Dernière Vague and the Rise of Discourse combined to exalt Ashbery to a prominence that, back in the sixties, would have seemed preposterous (the same combination of forces that, significantly, failed to embrace the other New York poets with anything like the same enthusiasm). It was, of course, also the time Ashbery's poems had come into their serious discursive look, making possible their subsumption under respectable critical categories of psychological and spiritual Quest.

Let me add, parenthetically, that I find Barbara Guest to be a different story. Long eclipsed by the others, even around New York, she has come into her own in the 1980s, partly because the fragmented language and consciousness she has always worked with have become fashionable. As always, much of the current fashion is uninspired, lacking her artistic integrity, her artistic intelligence, and, to put it simply, her gift.

★ ★ ★

Before I saw my limb off in the manner of a Trevor Winkfield character, let me make a sort of point, or at least an indirect one. When I began to think about this impossible topic, what first came to mind was Frank O'Hara, the possibility that, whatever things were like in the general field of influences, some things might be different if he were alive. What do I mean, and am I simply being in some illogical way nostalgic? For one thing, that Ashbery's current influence would have some healthy competition. For another, that the sheer range of O'Hara's poetry (not merely the "I do this, I do that" poems) might be tapped to a far greater degree than it has been. For a third, that the vigor, which seems to me a fundamental health, implicit in the freedom with which he practiced and, on those rare occasions, preached—the opposite of a program—might be tonic, a Resurrectine. Going on your nerve gets some poets into trouble; but it remains, like the Projective Verse idea (which I've always found more similar to O'Hara's than not), not merely an inspiring way of writing but what in fact a great many good poets have always done, or even Donne. The form-antiform issue doesn't come up in O'Hara because he's everywhere a poet; he *proves* you can write a sonnet and still love Williams, be pissed off or outrageous—and elegant besides. Put "Easter," "Jane Awake," "To the Film Industry in Crisis," "To the Harbormaster," and "Second Avenue" side by side. There's so much room in his oeuvre for younger writers to move around in.

I met my first New York poet, Koch, a couple of months after O'Hara died. All I know about O'Hara's legendary presence I've heard from friends like Tony Towle, or read about. It seems at least possible that the force of his personality coupled with the force and variety of his work might have changed some of the New York influence field around, injected vitality where, though it's not often admitted, some vitality has been missing. Notice I haven't discussed the drying up of outlets for these influences even to show themselves, nor the largely hidden second generation (if it exists) which, dare I say it, represents a secret strength of American poetry, and my limb has just cracked.

Schuyler's Mighty Line
(with an Essay Question)

When James Schuyler's extraordinary 60-page poem "The Morning of the Poem" appeared in 1980, it marked the advent of his exceptionally long line: by the time the poem was halfway through, the lines had swelled to virtually two lines each. Although he clearly wasn't counting beats or syllables, there seemed to be a reason, however unstatable, for every break—not only the official breaks but, remarkably, the runovers as well. In other words, the lines *were* two lines each, as well as being single lines long enough to pass for prose. Within this roomy framework, which recalled Whitman, Schuyler established his own permissions to do pretty much as he pleased, traveling smoothly and confidently on the strength of his associations from one image or memory or aperçu to the next.

As often turns out to be the case, this outsize line had precursors in the poet's own work. "December" and "April and Its Forsythia" as well as several others from his early book *Freely Espousing* have lines that extend beyond the margin. The splendid title poems of his next two books, the 6-page "Crystal Lithium" and the 17-page "Hymn to Life," enlarged the scope of both poem and line, introducing what might be called his Ongoing Style—the format that eventually resulted in his monumental poems.

[A condensed version of this piece appeared in *Denver Quarterly*, Spring 1990]

Too cold to get up though at the edges of the blinds
                                                    [the sky
Shows blue as flames that break on a red sea in which
                                        [black coals float:
Pebbles in a pocket embed the seam with grains of sand
Which, as they will, have found their way into a
                            [pattern between foot and bedfoot
"A place for everything and everything in its place"
                                [how wasteful, how wrong
It seems when snow in fat, hand-stuffed flakes falls
                                [slow and steady in the sea
"Now you see it, now you don't" the waves growl as they
                                            [grind ashore...
            [*The Crystal Lithium*, p. 66]

The colon ending the second line above and the absence of either
punctuation or connective word between the fourth and fifth lines
are of the essence: two of Schuyler's means, both within and outside
his lengthy lines, to keep a poem going. The colons, in particular,
increasingly serve to push the long poems ahead. As often as not a
colon represents a large "as if": it is as if this follows from that (it
may, but it may not). Without stanza breaks, with innocent-looking
initial capitals and periods wrapping up what are in fact disjunc-
tions, the lines look conventional and even prose-like on the page—
but that is the last thing they are.

As lengthy as lines get in "The Crystal Lithium" and "Hymn to
Life," it isn't until "The Morning of the Poem" that they begin to
run over apparently on purpose, even, as in the first half of the
poem, traversing the carriage return before absolutely necessary:

111

The exhalation of Baudelaire's image of
    terror which is
Not terror but the artist's (your) determination
    to be strong
To see things as they are too fierce and yet
    not too much: in
Western New York, why Baudelaire? In Chelsea,
    why not? Smile,
July day. Why did Baudelaire wander in? Don't
    I love Heine more? Or
Walt Whitman, Walt? No, they come to my death-
    bed and one by one take my hand
And say, "So long, old man," and who was it
    who in the Café Montana told,
In all seriousness, that the triumph of Mrs S.,
    future Duchess of W., was that
"They say she's a circus in bed." I like to
    dwell on that, the caged lions
And the whips, ball-balancing seals, "And now,
    without a net..."
        [*The Morning of the Poem*, pp. 58-59]

I like to dwell on that too, along with the rest of this wonderful passage. I would also defend each official line break and each unofficial runover to my dying day.

One could, if one were so inclined, calculate what percentage of Schuyler's lines split before the copula or after, how often he puts the important word at the beginning (as critics tell us poets do), how many lines split between preposition and object, or between modifer and noun (not how we were taught, but part of the impetus). But Schuyler's subtle unfoldings of music and meanings recoil from that sort of analysis.

> terror which is
>> Not terror but the artist's (your) determination
>>> to be strong
>
>>>> . . . .
>
>>>> in
>> Western New York, why Baudelaire? In Chelsea,
>>> why not? Smile,
> July day.

I don't know of any nomenclature to describe the effect of moving from "is" down and left to "Not terror" or from "Smile" to "July Day." But I know each feels absolutely right. Not that one must consciously attend to each break, but that noticing how, for example, the curve of a particular cadence fits or doesn't exactly fit the shape or length of a line provides—I want to say a unique pleasure; at the least, a rare one involving ear, eye and even viscera. One *feels* a line reach a stopping point, then one feels it continue on.

2

One of the striking aspects of Schuyler's mastery is precisely that it is demonstrable in outsize lines and in poems that go on for half a book (not only "The Morning of the Poem" but the more recent "A Few Days" as well). What other poets who operate in similarly open territory—Whitman, Ginsberg, Ashbery, Koch, Ammons— have line breaks on their minds? One thinks, instead, of Elizabeth Bishop's beautifully crafted lines, and of Robert Creeley, whose

113

early poems insisted on their divisions. I think, too, of Frank O'Hara and of David Schubert, whose seemingly casual lineation masks a knowing, muscular manipulation of the reader's eye and ear. While Schuyler's lineation shares qualities with that of each of these poets, no one, it seems to me, displays his skill and resourcefulness in poems ranging from the thinnest lines to the fattest imaginable.

Early on, in an uncharacteristic villanelle, Schuyler showed what he could do with iambic pentameter:

> I do not always understand what you say.
> Once, when you said, across, you meant along.
> What is, is by its nature, on display.
>
> Words' meanings count, aside from what they weigh:
> poetry, like music, is not just song.
> I do not always understand what you say.
>
> [*The Home Book,* p. 8]

His poems in *Freely Espousing* mixed long lines and very short ones. The opening of his understated and moving elegy for Frank O'Hara, "Buried at Springs," has always struck me as a pinnacle of the art of line:

> There is a hornet in the room
> and one of us will have to go
> out the window into the late
> August midafternoon sun. I
> won. There is a certain challenge
> in being humane to hornets
> but not much. A launch draws
> two lines of wake behind it...
>
> [*Freely Espousing,* p. 89]

Lineation is of the essence here. Beginning with a deceptively conventional four-beat line, Schuyler goes on to play against it with increasing feeling and force. Nothing appears contrived, and yet the variety of effects is remarkable. Frequently in the early poems Schuyler will set up a basic rhythmic pattern and then, as it were, step out into the poem, departing from the pattern at will. The beautiful, resonant "Salute" is equally memorable for the subtle ease, efficacy, and centrality of its line breaks.

> Past is past, and if one
> remembers what one meant
> to do and never did, is
> not to have thought to do
> enough? Like that gather-
> ing of one of each I
> planned, to gather one
> of each kind of clover,
> daisy, paintbrush that
> grew in that field
> the cabin stood in and
> study them one afternoon
> before they wilted. Past
> is past. I salute
> that various field.

[*Freely Espousing,* p. 92]

What I mean to emphasize is that in all of Schuyler's books, the "skinny" (his term) poems are as masterful as the fattest: his short lines are not less mighty than the long ones. Among the gems in *The Crystal Lithium,* which somehow remains his central book in

115

spite of the expanded scope of the later work, is the extraordinarily skinny "Verge."

> A man cuts brush
> and piles it
> for a fire where
> fireweed will flower
> maybe, one day.
> All the leaves
> are down except
> the few that aren't.
> They shake or
> a wind shakes
> them but they
> won't go oh
> no there goes
> one now. No.
> It's a bird
> batting by...
>
> [*The Crystal Lithium,* pp. 56–57]

Beginnings, endings, and middles—along with internal and external rimes—are more obvious here than in the hyperspace of the very long poems with their vast amounts of information, but the essential workings are not, I think, different. The little jolts of pleasure, the surprises—and by contrast, how often one *relaxes* into other poets' work—come in virtually every line.

Finally, there are poems seemingly too narrow to remain standing (which they proudly do), such as "Buttered Greens," which closes

116

all done

not by

us or for

us but

with us

and within

the body

of a house

the frame

of wood or

bone it is

much the

same

[*Hymn To Life,* pp. 56–57]

Who else can take monometer, albeit a loose version, seriously and convince us to do the same? Schuyler can employ these skinniest of lines in love poems as well. And he can, when he chooses, produce exemplary end-stoppings to go along with all the enjambment, as in the simple-sentence music of "The Cenotaph" [*The Crystal Lithium*] or his lovely "Song" [*The Morning of the Poem*].

★ ★ ★

Footnote (Essay Question). There is little writing as exquisite as Schuyler's nature diaries in prose. How does that square with a focus on his poetic line? To me, it serves to underline the particular pleasures to be gained from his poems, whose lineation is among the things that mark him as one of our best poets by far—as well as one whose mastery seems unusually poetic, however unfashionable it is to say so.

COMMENTARY FOR *JOE SOAP'S CANOE*

Most of the time, at least when I think I'm writing well, I don't quite know what I'm after: I hope to surprise myself. Sometimes I have a tone or kind of language, or even a vague shape or length, before I start, but these often get shifted around before the poem is done. Sometimes I have a "wonderful" title or idea—which of course doesn't always pan out. A couple of examples: "Two Architectural Poems," "April," "Tinker to Evers to Randomness" and a couple of others from *The Year of the Olive Oil* were inspired partly by an idea of making lyrical poems out of material and language that had no business being lyrical. I think of these as Technical Lyrics. "Prometheus at Fenway" got its title from some art reviewing I was doing at the time, got going as a parody, and then to my surprise became a lot more serious.

Now the specific commentary you asked for. About twenty years ago, I visited Keats's house at Hampstead Heath and brought back Keats paperweights (!) for my poet friends Tony Towle and Paul Violi. Ten years after that, it occurred to me to make a "paperweight" of words for the neglected poet William Cowper, whose long poem "The Task" I had recently read and been very moved by. I was inspired by the idea of making critical-sounding talk into a poem— not including critical remarks in a poem but making the criticism equal the poem (at least a part of it); I know I was more interested, at

---

[*Joe Soap's Canoe,* 1991]

least initially, in that idea than in writing about Cowper.

As part of the paperweight idea, I originally tried to shape the poem into a circle (how's that for formalism). I also wanted, and kept, a substantial quotation from Cowper's poem in my poem, and I wanted it to come in without warning at the very end, in one sense turning all that preceded into an introduction (somewhat like the explanatory material on a museum wall next to a piece of sculpture, or a paperweight). A secret pleasure was quoting him at his most rapt, after calling him non-rapturous and non-rhapsodic.

By the way, in accepting "For a Cowper Paperweight" a few years ago, the poetry editor of *The Paris Review* suggested that the quotation could be cut some! (I didn't go along with it.) To me, the inappropriate length, not that it's so long, constituted a breaking of the rules, one of the things that made the poem a poem and not an academic piece, which in some non-humorous way it was also parodying. As I write about it, this rule-breaking doesn't sound very daring. But I find that I produce things I like when I start out, at least, to do something uncalled for, even outrageous, if only to me.

LEAPING & CREEPING: SEVERAL LECTURES

One of the first things the large topic "The State of the Art" set me to puzzling over is why, exactly, given its competence and sophistication, so little of the poetry around is satisfying, let alone exciting. A part of it, I'm sure, has to do with what is sometimes called the "prevailing style"—the poetic vernacular (which can have varying accents, one of which would include various academic torturings), tried and true, readily available for use, encompassing language, nature and range of subjects, decorum level, ambitions, and so on. For quite a while, in America, what has prevailed has been a non-adventurous poetry, quotidian, often domestic, linguistically transparent. The prevailing style co-exists with and sometimes overlaps, if I have the idea right, the salient poetic movements of the time, although it occupies the much vaster stretches in between. Sometimes, particularly in the case of subject-oriented movements, it maintains a subtle stronghold on the poetics end regardless of the editorial policy. It survives and thrives, often pretending that the more visible poetries either don't exist or don't matter. Self-perpetuation via the institutional wards, the PSA, the YMHA, the New York reviewers, the college anthologies (whose role in all this isn't sufficiently acknowledged), and the workshop-spawned workshops,

---

[Presented at The Poetry Project Symposium on "The State of the Art," May 1991; printed in *American Poetry Review*, January–February 1992]

is just about guaranteed. In equal and opposite reactions, those poets who see themselves outside this framework, say nearly everyone here, often pretend things aren't as they are, or acknowledge the situation while dismissing its significance, or, when it's just too infuriating, spend a lot of their energies in anger.

As has been well documented, the current poetry world, small as it is, is a series of poetry worlds which operate largely in and on their own terms and collide mostly in mutterings, sotto voce. They might be pictured in the old image of concentric spheres, with the prevailing stylers at the center (or, conceivably, at the far-off but constant reaches of the fixed stars), and the other worlds whirling at varying distances from the center. The celestial music, if any, is hard to hear. There are different ways to draw the map. I recall a college poetry text that presumed to draw a poets star chart, with first magnitude figures in larger type, on out to the marginal, or New York, poets. Talk about canon (and whistling in the dark). This is all what used to be called the literary situation, the sociology and politics and economics of literary influence, but I think it has a good deal to do with the state of the art.

Now I'm going to make a leap. Along with the prevailing style in American poetry, which transcends, or more accurately embraces, current issues of gender, ethnicity, sexuality, logocentrism, economic determinants, etc. (which, by the way, suggests that the MFA is the Lost Ark of deconstruction), has grown up—on a smaller scale to be sure—a newly prevailing post-structuralist parataxis. Prevailing not in the vast sphere of the tried and true but in allegedly advanced circles. Just as there are presses and publications that can be depended upon to rehearse the prevailing style, there are those that present the paratactic poetic in a representative way. I'm generalizing, of course. By paratactics I mean poems—or texts in magazines

121

contributed to and read by poets—that make a point of eliminating connections, conjunctions and transitions in favor of extreme unconnectedness: often a kind of domino structure, coupled with an overall indeterminacy of meaning, perhaps influenced by recent Theory's focus on the evils of closure. Much of this writing looks as much like prose as it looks like poetry; much of it is fragmented. If one read only these publications, one could well think that the current state of the art is Parataxis in a rather large sense.

This is James Schuyler's poem "Light From Canada."

> A wonderful freshness, air
> that billows like bedsheets
> on a clothesline and the clouds
> hang in a traffic jam: summer
> heads home. Evangeline,
> our light is scoured and Nova
> Scotian and of a clarity that
> opens up the huddled masses
> of the stolid spruce so you
> see them in their bristling
> individuality. The other
> day, walking among them, I
> cast my gaze upon the ground
> in hope of orchids and,
> pendant, dead, a sharp shadow
> in the shade, a branch gouged
> and left me "scarred forever
> 'neath the eye." Not quite. Not
> the cut, but the surprise, and
> how, when her dress caught fire,
> Longfellow's wife spun

into his arms and in the dying
of its flaring, died. The
irreparable, which changes
nothing that went before
though it ends it. Above the wash
and bark of rumpled water, a gull
falls down the wind to dine
on fish that swim up to do same.

Surprise, whether engendered by an absence of transitional markers or fragmentation of the usual coherencies or a leap to a new tone, attitude, subject, diction, figure, idea, and so on, has always been a poetic resource, sometimes the closest thing to magic—"and / how, when her dress caught fire, / Longfellow's wife spun / into his arms and in the dying / of its flaring, died." And how; the "and how" in this case being a false conjunction that stuns by its illogicality. Similarly, when Emily Dickinson in the middle of describing what it's like to be human and having to face winter—what the light looks and feels like to us as creatures both connected to and disconnected from the landscape (at least since 1798)—arrives suddenly at "the Distance/ On the look of Death," that arrival is a stunning leap into hyperspace: the sphere, our unpoetic one, has suddenly slowed almost to a stop: one is a part of what is transcendent. I could, I think, maintain that all exciting poetry has something of this surprise element, this apparently magical leaping from order to a higher disorder because born somehow out of nothing that could have been foreseen—but it would be hard to make the case in terms that strong.

Consider these lines from an early poem by John Ashbery:

These lacustrine cities grew out of loathing
Into something forgetful, although angry with history.

They are the product of an idea: that man is horrible,
    for instance,
Though this is only one example.

Here the leaps, or surprising turns, come so rapidly in such a small space that it's almost impossible to stay on board. Yet we have come to accept the holding on, for dear life as it were, as a condition of 20th-century art. We try, to the extent that we can, to follow and participate, and in the vortex of poetic forces and meanings we emerge—if we are fortunate—with an exciting and memorable experience, different in the case of Ashbery's poem from the memorable experiences to be gained from "A Certain Slant of Light," or "The Wasteland," or Rimbaud's "Illuminations" (or for that matter Walter Benjamin's) in some respects but not all.

I find, speaking for myself, or as the baseball announcers say, This is Ralph Kiner saying this is Ralph Kiner, a striking contrast between these poems that employ leaps and much of the prevailing paratactics. Whereas one attends to "These Lacustrine Cities" despite the threat seemingly to one's *capacity to read,* out of a belief that not attending would diminish one as a reader and also diminish the art which has suddenly and stunningly been enlarged, there is missing in much—not all—of the writing I am referring to the sense that attending is crucial. I don't know how exactly to demonstrate this, or that it can be demonstrated—that's the problem of criticism as well as the glory of the arts. Charles Bernstein states it in rather blunt terms at the conclusion to his *Artifice of Absorption:* "are we putting / each other to sleep / or waking each other up; / & what do we wake to?" I would add that it depends on which alarm clock you consult. I'm very much aware that taste, value judgments and the like are highly suspect in some circles as having no normative force whatsoever, merely bespeaking the markings of whatever groups and forces went into the formation of one's pre-conceptions—though I must say that I discern in those same circles a willingness to consider some works, and some writers, far more important than others. Perhaps, with this new writing, it's a case of too many leaps eroding the cliff (the Gloucester syndrome); or too many jolts amounting in the end to no jolt despite the legitimate need to charge up dead batteries—like, to switch the figure, floating through the day on a case of beer: there is a buzz, but not often the excitement poetry, of all the linguistic arts, has from time to time seemed capable of. Not by any means that we must revert to the decorum of syntax—but that disjunction, with or without fragmentation, doesn't appear to constitute a be-all and end-all, a substitute for the numerous ways poetry can operate. Perhaps ultimately it's the rather familiar phenomenon of discovery hardening over time, and sometimes a short time, into codification, whether the discovery has to do with an English Romantic man speaking to English Romantic men, or "I do this I do that" (as Frank O'Hara described the internal progress of certain of his poems), or, more recently, the play of signifiers. Agendas have a way of producing such growth patterns. What begins as, or continues to be in theory, an extension turns out to be a narrowing down—in much the same way, I would suggest, that confining texts to the problematics of meaning is a severe limitation on the critical/theoretical end. I hasten to add that there are exceptions.

It would appear to boil down to what you want, what we want, from art. As James Schuyler bluntly and resonantly puts it in one of his Payne Whitney poems, "What is a / poem, anyway." Critics, traditionally, have wanted something other than a poem. Metacritics have traditionally practiced philosophy in a narrow confine. Theory is looking more and more like the intellectual jazz of the end-of-century, and not caring much (as jazz did in the fifties) about a return to the tune. The general reader, if that abstraction still makes sense, no longer has much to say or a place to say it. I'm half joking, as I have been interested in all these approaches. But the other half has to do with the state of the art, poetry, as in, Where's the poetry, and who genuinely cares about it these days apart from what it can be made to state or represent or divulge or generate? I'll leave those questions hanging: Where's the poetry? Who genuinely cares about it?

I notice, rereading what I've written, that the term "exciting" appears a few times as though a designated substitute for more obviously objectionable terms these days like "good" or "great." As though poems I read more than once tend to have something in common with Michael Jordan. I could have used "important" instead; but I find that I dislike that idea: the important, the "major" poets, are not invariably the most inspiring, and morevoer conspire to keep exciting poets out of the Norton anthologies. "Interesting" is all right if too indulgent, a little easy-going—still, better than exciting if exciting primarily suggests loud, those poems that startle but don't satisfy. Exciting is all right so long as poets such as John Clare, Lorine Niedecker, and Mei-mei Berssenbrugge come to mind along with the slam-dunkers. What I mean to say is that Anatoly Karpov is as brilliant as Gary Kasparov. This is all personal opinion.

In the first book of *Gulliver's Travels,* Gulliver is informed that Lilliputians compete for royal favors by leaping and creeping—I like the phrase—over and under a stick, an Enlightenment limbo. If so-called advanced writing these days is notable for its leaps, its nonlinearity, what is often referred to as academic poetry (which isn't confined to poets who teach) generally creeps, the opposite of genuine risk-taking. Academic poetry rarely rises to the top of its banks and never overflows them, following various well-worn channels of decorum, the more invidious of which seem to me to involve subjects and attitudes more than the usual whipping boys of rime, meter, and traditional form. There is a more interesting sense of creeping. A poem that inches its way along, as certain Robert Creeley poems may be said to do, can simultaneously perform exciting leaps. Slow pace, small size, groping one's way can all be exciting, despite the critical predilection for the big statement as guarantee of the important poet: I am serious and aspiring in a large format, therefore I am to be taken seriously, which means written about, placed, connected to my literary connections. To creep, in this sense, is simply to move in the poem in a different way, to structure the poetic space differently. In some ways a combination of leaping and creeping can be all the more stunning, as when one becomes context for the other. Not merely does subtlety pack force still, but at its best it can give the lie to programs and agendas, restore to art its capacity for magic.

In grappling with the notion of state of the art, I find that it is *states* plural that are most meaningful. One state of the art has to do with its mode of being: what a poem is, where exactly it is to be found (page, auditorium, reader's head, all readers, etc.), how it functions and what it conceals, and so on. This area has been "foregrounded" by theorists. Another current meaning is normative, specifically "most advanced," as in state-of-the-art word processing. (See Hammacher-Schlemmer catalogs for a series of clever parodies of this meaning of state of the art.) A third meaning refers to the condition, including the presumed health, of the art as a whole, here or wherever. Apart from the fragmented poetry world, this would include *status*, as in government priorities, budget cuts, importance relative to other public matters such as fear of obscenity, neighborhood theaters that present short stories (but not poems) as if they were theater. It also involves judgments as to how poetry, in our case, is doing. Remember Ed Koch? Picture him dressed up as the Muse and button-holing anyone who will listen. Is there or isn't there as much exciting work being done now as there was in the fifties and sixties? There are less important meanings for state of the art too: New York, California, Illinois, and New Jersey, for example; even conceivably an ideal state created by and for poetry: the State of the Art of Poetry, a utopian community on the banks of the Susquehanna River. As to the issues implicit in each of these senses of the term I would say it depends on whom you ask—this is the state of art, after all, you wouldn't expect anyone's annual address to satisfy more than a handful. I would add, parenthetically, that the object of the preposition has its meanings as well. If you take art, as I don't think we do most of the time, as normative, then by definition some, if not all according to the third meaning above, is well. If the term is entirely descriptive, then health is a legitimate if problematic concern, although probably no mortal is qualified to proclaim the health of any art that exists at the same time he or she does. As for state as in chemical state, it seems to me to go without saying that poetry is always and forever volatile.

We have learned from ethnic, sexual and other deconstructing analyses of literary works—although, if you've noticed, poetry, what we're presumably interested in, is rarely acknowledged by Theory let alone dealt with fairly and squarely—that not only is no point of view objective, but that the subjectivity of any point of view has numerous underpinnings, some of them invidious. No one escapes his/her markings. Hence the frequency in discourse of terms like foregrounding, privileging, marginalizing, spatial metaphors that presumably keep everything on a descriptive, relative level. And then something curious follows, or doesn't quite follow: there is still art, and the feeling that some of it is more important, or less easy to forget or to look away from, or simply better than other art. Taste, like tin ears, is not easy to legislate out of existence. Speaking for myself, I feel that State of the Art in the ontological sense is an interesting, largely philosophical subject, formerly the province of aestheticians, that in our age of theory has been foregrounded at the expense of poetry; that state-of-the-art poetry consists, always, of those poems that seem to a given reader to be the most exciting, whenever, wherever, or about whatever they were written; that the health of poetry hereabouts, while needing to be determined by every onlooker, is a supremely mixed bag: a vast amount of dullness, unwitting repetition of the past, and party line rewarded by dull-seeking prize-givers, but, as always, at least within many of the definable spheres, some exciting writers; that no geographically determined state as of this evening is any more poetic than any other state, with the possible exception of Florida which Elizabeth Bishop called "the state with the prettiest name"; and that creating an artificial ideal state of whatever art, Yaddo writ large, would probably do more than anything imaginable to eventually do in the art.

Things don't, in fact, look all that good, despite exhilaration in some quarters that so much poetry is being written, and the number of literary newsletters now as compared, say, to the fifties. Those who profess to care about the arts never quite include the private arts in their largess (a secret reason for the rise in performance poetry?). Big-press publishing, traditionally mirroring the vastly disproportionate percentages of inconsequential vs. exciting poetry, now handles far less poetry of any kind. The official poetry organs and organisms seem to me largely baleful in their wide-ranging hegemony. And in the sphere where poetry is supposed to matter most, ideas about it continue to distort it and its reasons for being, with French-induced habits of mind intensifying the critical disregard that has been going on for a long time. One still wants to say, "Yes. And—?" (This is the Yes-And Principle.) Yes, I see, and so—? So the poetry is—? So we read the poem because—? So you're considering *poetry* because you feel that it—?

And the genuine stuff, to sneak in at least one other value-laden term, is in as short supply as ever—as, one might add, are the proportions of Coleridge to Coleridge and Laura Riding to Laura Riding Jackson. What else is new. I like, by the way, to think of myself as being as much in favor of the new as anyone. A poet friend said recently that it's good that poetry is back underground. I'm not so sure about the "back," but clearly he meant our kind of poetry, whatever that is—presumably the kind that isn't getting much notice! It seems to me that the genuine article is, to some significant degree, always underground. A case could be made for the essential (value-laden) John Ashbery remaining underground during his award years, the above-ground Ashbery being largely critical rather than poetic territory. To make another small leap—what is a critic, anyway. A. The subject for another lecture. But what a strange business criticism keeps demonstrating itself to be, spending so much of its time on meanings and issues like indeterminacy and closure, rather than on why this poem still gives you chills after your having known it almost by heart for twenty-five years. I know I'm conflating criticism and theory. One would think literature was of biblical status.—Or is the whole approach a subtle one that only pretends to value what isn't really valued very much. It's no wonder, to extend the leap just a little further, that students are flocking away from poetry, that English departments are under siege, and that the besiegers are perpetuating many of the existing problems on other

130

levels, deconstructing what oughtn't to have been construed, I should say merely construed, in the first place. As for poetry's being undergound, whether newly or not, if that's true it's certainly a double-edged situation. Even if it's good for poetry, it can't be that good for the poet. If it's paradoxically a sign of health, then few who have anything to do with the currently delineated poetry worlds can benefit from it. Still....

Poetry is rare, various, volatile, abstract (as Wallace Stevens has made clear), concrete (as William Carlos Williams has made clear), sometimes a matter of voice and authority, sometimes a matter of subjects, sometimes representative of a new conception of or connection to the self, sometimes a new way of putting elements of language together, sometimes in lines, sometimes in sentences, sometimes in paragraphs, sometimes fragmentary. Conceptual categories have an impossible time containing it or accounting for its genuineness when it appears genuine. Astonishing poems have been written in traditional forms, some of them employing closure (like mouths, plays, flies, and a lot of other things, one wonders why some poems can't be open and others closed), the form issue so-called being to my mind a straw man elevated on the one hand to rationalize anything that disrupts form, and on the other to rationalize a barrage of dull retrograde verse. It's hardly possible to imagine an exciting "formalist" poet these days—as opposed to an exciting poet like Elizabeth Bishop or Kenneth Koch or Jeremy Prynne who is occasionally inspired by a formal challenge. And then someone like Bernadette Mayer comes along and, in her wonderful *Sonnets,* extends not only formal poetry but the state of the art.

In short, which this no longer seems as it did when I was worrying how to fill fifteen minutes, I see the various attempts to limit what poetry can or should be or do as the continuing opposition—

in an age of theory that includes theory. I almost said enemy, but that seems to me to lose in perspective what it gains in emotional content. In our involvement with poetry, and I guess I've made it plain that I think of poems rather than texts regardless of how difficult the lines are to draw, do we really want to elevate our analytical and intellectual selves to such an extent over our emotional selves? Is poetics conceivably more exciting than poetry? I know there are many issues, explicit and otherwise, in what I've said. In closing, let me emphasize the importance of trying, at least, to take art on its own terms. Perceiving an intention, even if that means faking one in a strictly philosophical sense, seems to me a lot less invidious and a lot more useful than surrounding poetry with programs and concepts that discourage both it and its reception. In any case, these are a few of the things the general rubric State of the Art suggested.

SEVEN DAYS IN JULY

for Bill Corbett (and JS)

7/9

Has the *chicory* done any writing lately?

7/19

The ghostly cat belonging to the neighbor who is away killed one
of the two swallows that had been fond of perching on the pruned
nubs of the lilac bush. We all had a front-row view. After disappear-
ing with the carcass he rematerialized around dusk lying in wait for
something (dessert?) just at the edge of the unmown grass. Eerily
the moon, at about the same time, appeared to be losing shape or
somehow changing it radically, as though the bag that normally
houses it had had its drawstring loosened, permitting gravity (and
distortion) for once to operate. Moon, cat, breasts, Queen Anne's
Lace, a few newly mown stars all lying on the lawn underneath
hazy cloud cover.

7/25

If there is nothing outside the window but the swamp maple-in-
itself, and nothing inside but the pen writing as it writes, then the
glow of the new leaves is a phenomenon of which, if I have knowl-

[*That Various Field for James Schuyler,* edited by William Corbett &
Geoffrey Young (The Figures, 1991)]

edge I can't say, and if I don't I can't know it apart from the leaves themselves, which appear to magnetize the declining sun every afternoon and pull it through quantities of unspeakably charged states of being.

7/26
The ten stages of reality: landscape, distance, figment, evanescence, youth, the collective unconscious, perspicacity, dusk, logic, ground cover.

7/28
The Villa Rotunda of days (would be nice right about now).

(Who was it who said, "My daughter is a lucky man she has me for a father?")

7/29
What would be lost if (as happens to be the case) the writing adds *nothing,* neither does it subtract from the sum total of experiences the day has entirely on its own? What about the housefly and *its* short "writing life," screened in or screened out...Romantic spiders, Neoclassical bumblebees, Symbolist and occasionally Cubist-leaning hornets, Surrealist fireflies...the Criticism of mosquitoes...

7/31
Real wind, not breeze, during the afternoon, leaving early evening adrift about ten feet from the shore waving its arms, but calmly, aware of an inner strength. The dull slate blue of the hills is what seawater might look like if a storm cloud were suddenly dipped into it.

(date lost)

As though drill bits of sky had broken off and, in addition to losing almost all function, had acquired a rather cold greenish tone as they approached closer to earth—

TONY TOWLE'S NEW YORK POEMS

One of the ironies of American poetry is that many of its best poets seem to require rediscovering. Tony Towle's book *North*, containing his early New York poems, won the prestigious Frank O'Hara Award in 1970. The award, named for the wonderful New York poet who died in a tragic accident at the age of 40, was established to encourage "experimental poetry," then as now in much need of encouragement; in the case of *North* the O'Hara Foundation was recognizing the work of one of the most original and gifted young poets in the country. Not altogether surprisingly, the book received only limited attention outside New York City, where both O'Hara and Towle lived, published their poems and gave readings. Even there, Towle's reputation was confined to the relatively small group of poets and admirers of the so-called New York School, whose poetics and practice seemed to provoke the rest of the country.

The situation for poetry, particularly of the experimental kind, has if anything worsened in the intervening decades. Bad poetry has driven out good in many places where readers go to look for it. Whereas in the 1950s and 1960s there was a real sense of an avant-garde—composed of several factions (New York, Beats, Black Mountain) but united against the evils of a poetic Establishment—there now seems, even among "advanced" groups, an atmosphere of prickly isolationism. On top of this, Theory has encroached on

[1992]

what used to be largely poetic territory to an extent that would have been incomprehensible in the 1950s and 1960s. It's not only hard to find the genuine article, it's hard to get one's bearings.

Out of print for much too long, these beautiful lyrical poems represent the half-decade, 1965-1970, when Towle's early experiments with form, voice, language, tone, etc., came together to define him as a poet. They are not, at first blush, easy poems to grasp. Intensely personal, even Romantic, they are simultaneously modernist through and through. They pay lip service, as it were, to a number of poetic conventions (unlike so much contemporary poetry, which makes a point of jettisoning conventions entirely) while ultimately flouting them: their cohesive look masks a pervasive and frequently enigmatic disjunction featuring surreal and cinematic jumps, dramatic shifts in voice, narrative that doesn't add up, strings of participial phrases that don't clearly refer, false parallels, and the like. Yet the poems have an extraordinary depth of feeling. Another New York poet remarked to me some years ago that of all the poems he continued to read, Tony's were the ones that invariably moved him to tears.

Towle has a Keats or even a Shelley side which sets him well apart from his contemporaries. These *are* New York poems, by a witty and highly sophisticated New Yorker whose sophistication takes in grubby local politics as well as the history of poetry and history in general; but in true Romantic fashion their true locus is the poet's Self, writ large. They are self-conscious in just about every sense of the term, even to self-indulgence. Moreover they have an uncanny way of treating fundamentally vague and ethereal matters as though they were concrete. Towle's decidedly un-William Carlos Williams-like predilection is for elevated tone, lush imagery, extravagant metaphor, and ornate syntax. But he can descend, in the space

of a single line, to a pure Williams (if not Jimmy Breslin) colloquial-
ism, as in the poem "Daybreak" where the Muse—who makes few
if any appearances these days—enters the poet's bedroom "stutter-
ing." The poems' Romantic flights are undercut by the poet's knowing wit. Both texture and flavor seem to me unique in modern
poetry.

Although people don't cease to complain about it, difficulty so-
called is with us to stay, if we care about contemporary art. Some of
the difficulty in grasping Towle's work is unavoidable, as it is, for
example, with Gongora, who stands somewhere behind these
poems. (On the other hand and much to the point are the influence
of Whitman and O'Hara. Towle clearly operates on colossal
"nerve"—O'Hara's term. Whereas O'Hara sometimes wrote what
he called "I do this I do that" poems, Towle's procedure is something like "I do this I *think* that, now I *am* that, now that has
become *this,* now I'm considering what I just thought and felt
about that, etc.) A good deal of the apparent difficulty vanishes
with the understanding that the poems aim at other things besides
discursive meanings alone. T. S. Eliot once acknowledged that his
poetic decisions were "quasi-musical" ones; I think the same is sub-
stantially true for Towle. Music in fact permeates his poetry. In one
poem he compares his work to that of Poulenc and Satie (though
his own wit strikes me as darker and less playful). More importantly,
he organizes his materials much more in the manner of music than
in the manner of either discursive prose or conventional verse, from
his word choices and syntactical structures to cadencings and trans-
positions and counterpointings. Frequently a new stanza appears to
begin the poem anew, the way a movement does a symphony.

It would be hard to say that these New York poems are happy
poems. For all their wit and genuine humor as well, the predomi-

nant tone is elegiac. They confront the human condition, in particular its darker aspects—restlessness and restless desire, intermittent disorientation and frustration, even despair—in a much more direct way than most current poetry, which characteristically limits itself either to dailiness (one of the strains in Towle's work) or to language-play. And yet the poems are exhilarating, some of the most beautiful to come out of a genuinely exciting time in American poetry.

STATEMENT FOR *PATAPHYSICS*

Dear Yanni and Leo,

I'm sure moments of "arrival" are indeed critical, as you suggest, but I find it virtually impossible to pinpoint them. Frequently I dredge up poems that have been lying around in one form or another for months or even years—when is the arrival time? Departures, unfortunately, are a lot easier to figure out. My feeling is that "moments" applies to single poems as much as to poems in general.

—Just by way of footnote, I'd add that my (few) efforts to describe what I'm working on have invariably interfered, to put it at its mildest, with what I'm working on. I wish it were otherwise!

Best wishes,

[*Pataphysics,* 1993]

JOHN HOLLANDER'S *TYPES OF SHAPE*

This is an exceptionally clever little book of "emblematic," or shaped, poems, ranging from more or less familiar shapes like cats and a lightbulb to inspiredly complicated ones like a beach umbrella together with its shadow (and pole consisting of one 2-letter word per line), a note on lined music paper, the domed Low Library at Columbia, and—my favorites—two on adjoining pages: an arrow that meditates on its own existence, while pointing ahead to the silhouette of New York State on the next page, the occasion for a new meditation. The challenge of the form is immense, virtually impossible; and by demonstrating not only that shape and "meaning" can be tied together in non-trivial ways (putting light years, let's say, between these and so-called "concrete poems") but that the genre can include poems that are lyrical and even philosophical, in addition to being handsome and ingenious, Hollander deserves a niche in the Cathedral of Poetry. In fact, he's made the territory so much his own, Apollinaire and Herbert notwithstanding, it's hard to imagine what else might follow.

The premise does, like most formal ideas, have its built-in limitations and pitfalls. For one, each shape demands the sustaining of an original inspiration: no matter how brilliant the idea and the opening, you still have to finish out the prescribed shape. Hollander's openings and closings are invariably fresh and imaginative both the-

[*Poetry Project Newsletter,* February/March 1993]

matically and visually, satisfying the formal half of the challenge; middles are occasionally a problem. The rigors of adhering to the silhouette produce some uninspired writing, a lyricism too easily arrived at (at least for my taste); also some straining after meaning, or Meaningfulness, as if to convince the reader that this is after all a serious game.

But all in all, there is a great deal of pleasure to be gained from watching these poems work out their premises, sometimes traveling a good distance in the process—and from watching Hollander, who is nothing if not deft as well as erudite, think and feel his way through the metaphysics, erotics and aesthetics, as well as the sheer landscapes and weather, of living. Remarkably, in the best poems the shapes do seem to *be* and speak for (or about) themselves. Not only does the book give ingenuity a good name; it reaffirms the paradox that formal poetry, albeit in rare instances, can be inspiring and even liberating. I for one am left somewhat in awe.

Twenty-five of the poems in *Types of Shape* were originally collected in 1969 (where was I?—or rather, the '60s couldn't have been the best time for a book of formal poems); this reissue has ten new ones, an interesting and useful introduction covering the history of the genre and Hollander's own approach to it, and semi-scholarly notes (which probably don't need to be there) to each poem in the book.

Art in Its Own Terms:
Fairfield Porter's Critical Writing

I've always liked Frank O'Hara's lines to a critic:

> I cannot possibly think of you
> other than you are: the assassin
>
> of my orchards. You lurk there
> in the shadows, meting out
>
> conversation like Eve's first
> confusion between penises and
>
> snakes. Oh be droll, be jolly
> and be temperate! Do not
>
> frighten me more than you
> have to! I must live forever.

Granted, O'Hara was addressing a literary critic. But criticism, as they say, is criticism. We might disagree about who or what is to live forever, the artist or the art; but it's hard not to find O'Hara's stance appropriate.

Poetry Project Newsletter, October / November 1993]

Fairfield Porter is a lot better known these days as a painter than as a critic, though he wrote criticism on a fairly regular basis for 40 years, including a weekly art column for *The Nation*. As a critic, Porter is a singular, striking exception to O'Hara's rule. Porter brought to his writing a rare combination of talents and interests. He studied philosophy with Whitehead at Harvard and was interested also in the writings of Suzanne Langer, taking over ideas about the particularity of art from both. In addition to his passion for painting, he paid a good deal of attention to poetry. Well known for his blunt manner, he made this bluntness a virtue in his writing, saying only what he felt it necessary to say, refusing to "mete out conversation." Unlike so many aestheticians and theorists on the one hand and art writers on the other, he was at once a supremely attentive viewer and a clear, independent, and provocative thinker, responding directly and intuitively to individual works and frequently going on to formulate issues and implications in the widest terms—aesthetic, scientific, social, political. Rarest of all, his prose is not merely clear and precise but frequently beautiful.

Porter's interests as a reviewer and essayist cut across conventional boundaries. A figurative painter and one of the best, he was excited by abstraction he felt had *vitality* and dismayed by figurative painting that didn't. Though he had clear favorites among artists (Vuillard, Cornell, de Kooning), his thoughtful reviews range illuminatingly across a large body of the painting and sculpture of his time. His early interests in socialism and communism found their way into various pieces. If he found something he thought genuine he praised it; if not, he didn't pull his punch. What invariably provoked his disapproval, in and out of art, was what smacked of system or "scientific method"—the elevation of rules, concepts and categories above direct experience, a misguided approach he felt to be limiting

144

and ultimately destructive of the uniqueneness (inevitable arbitrari-
ness, surprise, mystery) of both art and life. Rackstraw Downes, in
his excellent introduction, narrates an incident that made an early
impression on Porter. Porter having introduced the critic Clement
Greenberg to de Kooning, Greenberg promptly scolded de Kooning for continuing to paint figuratively. De Kooning's reaction was,
"He wanted to be my boss, without pay." Porter concluded, "If that's
what he [Greenberg] says, I think I will do just exactly what he says
I can't do!" To Porter's independent, humanist way of thinking,
intellectual bosses (especially idea-oriented, prescriptive—and pro-
scriptive—critics) were the enemy.

Porter's method, by contrast, was to direct as much thoughtful
attention to his subject as he could. The critic's obligation was to
discover why and how the work succeeded or failed, in what its
vitality (or lack of it) lay. None of this precluded formulating issues
and implications, or making connections: Technology and Artistic
Perception, Intellect and Comedy, Reality and the Museum, etc.
Many of the short reviews move well beyond their occasions. One
might say that Porter's motto for things intellectual (following
William Carlos Williams' famous phrase "no ideas but in things") is,
no ideas but in some necessary and non-degrading relationship to
particulars. His aim was to appreciate, understand when *necessary*
(understanding and interpretation—except by analogy—do not
constitute the critical enterprise), remonstrate thoughtfully and
convincingly. His values come out loud and clear.

Art in Its Own Terms is a stimulating but moreover an inspiring
book: it makes one want to rush out to galleries (despite their currently dismal state) and it makes me want to write criticism. When
did that last happen? I can think of a dozen undergraduate and
graduate courses where this collection should be required reading.

In addition to the virtues of his prose, Porter's integrity as a thinker and the very quality of his attention are moving. Where his dislikes seem oddly pronounced, as for example in his negative remarks about Cezanne (or the Bauhaus or Constructivism or earthworks), they remain consonant with his consistently displayed values. No judgment or idea is dashed off, yet nothing is belabored. Porter's short reviews show as much care and thought as the longer pieces; among many others, those of the painters Albert York and Jon Schueler (barely half a page) are worth other critics' entire books.

This collection is a reprint, its original publication (Taplinger) having been in 1979, 4 years after Porter died. Both, needless to say, small presses. What, one can't help wondering, would Porter make of current fashions in criticism? My guess is that he would have a hard time thinking about the practitioners in other than Frank O'Hara's terms. How many of those who write with some connection to art or literature are genuinely appreciative, straightforward, unconfusing, "frightening" only where there is no alternative, temperate—let alone jolly or droll? With so much lately in the air about "completing" the work of the artist, it is Porter, it seems to me, who adds to the complex of art experience in the best and healthiest way, writing a richly human criticism that engages many concerns of artists and writers both.

Two or three items by way of footnote. 1) It's hard to imagine a better editor of Porter's prose than Rackstraw Downes, who in addition to being a wonderful painter himself shares many of Porter's values and critical strengths. 2) This being the *Poetry Project Newsletter,* it seems only mildly irrelevant to mention that Porter, in addition to being a painter and critic, wrote poems, was married to the poet Anne Channing, for an extended period housed the poet James Schuyler, and wrote prose, dare I say it, with a poet's strengths.

His piece on "Poets and Painters in Collaboration" contains illuminating, early appreciations of O'Hara, Schuyler, Koch and Ashbery. 3) One of Wallace Stevens' aphoristic "Adagia": "To a large extent, the problems of poets are the problems of painters and poets must often turn to the literature of painting for a discussion of their own problems." Not very often with beneficial results, but certainly here.

ON & FOR JIM BRODEY

(Memorial Reading at The Poetry Project, December 5, 1993)

One of the most memorable readings, at least from my point of view, occurred here in the 1970s. The place was jammed. The readers were Brodey and—I think: I may have blocked out some of it—Ginsberg. Brodey I barely knew, but I had always found his poetry inspiring. There I was sitting on the floor with a lot of other latecomers, listening to this poet I admired, when I began to hear—"as in a dream"—this elaborate poem evolve about Brodey's "Brunch at the Norths," along with Tony Towle, elegant drapery, crab meat "on green tissue," pâté—which Tony proceeded to form into balls and throw out the window—and the two of us, Paula and me, in ballet slippers and leotards (I had surprisingly cute legs) dancing, nibbling, and making conversation in these elegant surroundings. No matter that we lived on Broadway, this was Uptown. Clark Coolidge, who recently sent me a copy of the poem, said it struck him as "sounds of acid dropping amidst a Henry James tea party." I *think* I was smiling, nervously if so, as this long piece went along, somewhat flattered that we had been a part of Brodey's fantasy or dream or whatever, but really not knowing *how* to react, or how the rest of the big crowd would react, whether or not they knew us.

★ ★ ★

[Printed in *Lingo* 6, 1996]

Another Brodey Reading memory I have is of the two of us reading together at the Blue Mountain Gallery in the early '80s, and Brodey prefacing his half by stating that *his* poems were in *my* head all the time. Now, he knew that I admired his work. When we talked before the reading he told me how much he liked my poems and how well he knew them, and I responded by saying I knew some of his, too. It wasn't only the distortion and exaggeration that got me, it was that he would come out and *say* what he said. After all, I hadn't even begun my reading yet and here I was being presented as a disciple if not a worshipper!

Actually, we did form a little mutual admiration society, one of a number he had with fellow poets. He once announced to me that I came "directly" out of Schuyler and he came "directly" out of O'Hara. There's certainly some truth in that, but neither approaches the whole story. There's Schuyler in Brodey too; also, in different degrees and at different times, a lot of Ginsberg, Ceravolo, Berrigan, Rimbaud, Dylan Thomas (I think) and others. Even if you didn't know Jim well, you knew he was passionate about poetry and read tons of it, especially his contemporaries. He wrote often—possibly always—in response to the poetry he was reading. Sometimes you can spot Berrigan in a Brodey poem. In the early works like *Identikit,* there's a lot of Ceravolo, especially *Fits of Dawn.* Ginsberg seems to me to have been an abiding influence. Brodey's 300, or 400, or 1000—depending on whom you hear it from—poems with people's names as titles are not only a poetic gimmick; they're testimony to his involvement, if sometimes from a distance, with others, especially his fellow poets.

★ ★ ★

Brodey always seemed to me to have an immense talent, a genuine lyrical gift, which could get derailed or misplaced, leaving too many stunning fragments or flashes of poetry somewhere in the midst of what became for him a kind of post-Beat/Bebop shtick. When his song lines are permitted to really take off, when they don't get mired in, for example, his own personal reveling in the body and its countless orifices and productions—fixation is another way of looking at it—the poems soar. Interestingly the O'Hara that came to mind when I was thinking about Jim was "To the Harbor Master":

> I wanted to be sure to reach you;
> though my ship was on the way it got caught
> in some moorings. I am always tying up
> and then deciding to depart....

In Brodey's poems there's an ongoing wish to leave and reach, to transcend physical limitation—often via drugs and jazz, but also a genuine spiritual craving, I think—that all goes hand in hand with his reveling in or obsession with his low-down, physical self. There's a conflict of thrusts: up and out; and also down and out, and down and in (which sounds like football, another reveler in the high and the low). I also think of Williams in his "Danse Russe" (and I find it significant that the poems which come to mind are beautiful and lyrical ones), dancing naked and grotesquely before his mirror and singing "I am lonely, lonely./ I was born to be lonely,/ I am best so!" while admiring all the parts of his body. Brodey was lonely and driven, at least that's what the poems I've seen appear to indicate, and he is always turning back to his physical side or physical self for grounding. He gets caught in his own moorings; he swims in his own body fluids. But when it all works the poetry is really something. I hope this doesn't all sound *too* serious; his poetry isn't. In

150

Brodey at what I think is his best, homey details and language—a lot of which you just don't find in anyone else's poems—anchor the word and image flights in a successful way. I don't eat many "vomburgers" myself, but somehow Brodey makes the word, at least, appealing in his poems. I love the fact that he can talk about lust and "tushies" in the same line. If this is all fixation, oral or anal or both, it's also immediate and fresh, kids' stuff and not kids' stuff.

Brodey clearly knew how to make a capital P Poem as opposed to non-stop "juice and joy," but just as clearly he didn't care about making Poems a lot of the time, relying instead on strings of post-hipster phrases and language blips and riffs to take care of matters. I think he had a kind of ultimate faith in the power of poetry—in what the unconscious, given little or no direction, can do on its own. Too often, at least in my view, he over-indulged, in the unconscious as well as vomburgers, though terrific word combos and interesting *things* pop out all over the place. There is also a kind of centrifugal energy to his lines such that at times they threaten to leave both the poem and the page.

Of course this is only my take and, from what I've heard, most of us have seen only the tip of the iceberg. Two unpublished Brodey poems Coolidge recently mailed to me look better than a lot of what's already in print. And there are legends about the height of the Brodey stacks in Coolidge's basement.

10 ESSAYS FOR BARBARA GUEST

Wallace Stevens alleged, in one of his *Adagia*, that "poetry must resist the intelligence almost successfully." Although I've never been quite sure *whose* intelligence he was referring to, or exactly how to take the "must," I've always liked the remark. I like it partly because it seems to explain why certain poets, often my favorites, are scanted by the critical establishment. Their poetry resists the understanding; it escapes, at least to a significant extent, the conceptualizing ordinarily brought to bear on poetry by its organizers.

This is, admittedly, a *nice* way of looking at the critical neglect suffered by some of our best writers. There are, as everyone knows, other salient causes, mostly having to do with social currents and literary politics. But I do think Barbara Guest belongs to the group of significant resisters and escapers. It is certainly useful—her poems being increasingly difficult to grasp—to try to characterize her modes of writing; though I would argue strenuously that *grasp* is as much a matter of pointing, feeling, holding onto, as it is of cognition. From her earliest poems, which is to say from at least the 1950s, it was clear that shifts and leapings, not to speak of surreal atmospheres, were essential. Coherence in the usual sense was not an ambition. Yet it was also clear that the voice presenting the poems was entirely sure of itself; restless surface, interrupted narrative, fragmented landscape, and frequent disjunction somehow

_____

[Presented at Brown University, April 1994]

added up to a mysterious and resonant cohesiveness. I was originally going to title this piece "Con(Dis)-junction in Barbara Guest's Writing," in order to emphasize this mysterious holding together that, to my mind, continues to distinguish her writing from that of many of her contemporaries. By *not* throwing signifiers to the four winds in the hope, let us say, that they will prove as interesting as cloud formations; by situating her work in various ways on the tightrope—and I do mean to suggest risk—between traditional poetic materials and both modern and post-modern dismantlings, she has, it seems to me, produced one of the significant bodies of poetry in our time.

I'm by no means sure it's an issue for anyone but me and a few on this panel, but the notion of lyric poetry in our post-modern age is one that interests me a great deal both as a reader and a writer. I know it's not pressing in allegedly advanced circles. At the same time, the conventional lyric poem following what one might call "confessional" models continues to be vastly published and vastly promulgated in university writing programs (outside Rhode Island). I read Barbara's poetry as essentially lyrical. Recently it seems to me to be lyrical in a post-modern way, something of a paradox. In her New York period—as I expect it will come to be called, "New York School" or no "New York School"—the poetic self that felt, perceived, remembered, thought about "Stupid Physical Pain" and cooking dinner as well as aesthetics, narrated, depicted landscapes and interiors, was the locus of the poem. Not that it was fixed, or even at the center; if anything, the self was something of a hunter/gatherer of poetic materials, restlessly in motion, popping up to surprise, even splitting apart. Yet for all their non-linear movement and sophisticated offhandedness—both components of the early New York accent—the poems up to and including at least a

153

part of *Moscow Mansions* (1973), which seems to me a transitional book, had aims associated with the self or voice classically associated with lyrical poetry. They featured an "I," often in an immediate relation to its experience; they expressed strong feeling; they meant to be beautiful and affecting as well as modern and technically interesting; they produced a strong if progressively difficult and atonal music.

Neither this poetic self nor the aims of her earlier poetry have, it seems to me, been erased in Barbara's recent work. What has happened almost from book to book, which is to say gradually rather than suddenly, is that the basic lyric mode has undergone various dismantlings, transforming the texture of the poetry but not its essential nature. Feeling, "subject matter," narrative, referentiality all survive—but they do so mostly in fragments and traces. The self, pushed aside and below the surface, still insists on its right to be heard; its inner and outer life, once explicit as subject matter, now thread through and around pieces and stems and chunks of language. Sometimes "an emphasis falls on reality," as her wonderful phrase has it, sometimes not. In particular, the poems in *Fair Realism* and especially *Defensive Rapture* feature great spaces on the page, as though the poem was in fact the sky and the fragments of language, now clustering and now breaking apart, were fleeting intrusions on the order of gulls and passing clouds. What is striking is how much *feeling* cohabits with these marked and unmarked spaces. I find it illuminating that two of Barbara's favorite poets (who happen to be two of mine as well) are James Schuyler and the Cambridge [England] poet J. H. Prynne, the one seeming to be all observation, the other seemingly engrossed in language play. As always, appearances can be mightily deceiving.

Actually I think a case can be made for Barbara Guest as not only a post-modern lyric poet but as a post-modern Romantic—though I say that more softly. Faux narratives like "The Knight of the Swan," "Byron's Signatories," "The Turler Losses"; continual back-and-forth movement between landscape and interior life; exotic language and location; recurrent natural imagery, dailiness, etc., make this notion more suggestive, at least to me, than first appears. Another suggestive rubric that occurred to me in the course of thinking about Barbara's work as being equally involved with language and lyric is "Locating Things" (from an early book title: this is the business many of her poems both early and late seem to me to be about, with an equal emphasis on *locating* and on *things*). Others occurred to me too: Transformative Vocabularies (with a nod to Stevens, who I believe is a significant influence); Collaborating with the Poem; The Great Whereupon (great but mostly erased); Liquid Geometries (echoing her own two-term yokings of concrete and abstract); and Constructions of Surprise (a corollary, perhaps, of her not driving conventional expectation entirely out of the poem: the central surprise being that the poems retain an air of *construction* despite their continual, unexpected turns).

Barbara's poems are worth reading and rereading not because she was indeed a charter member of the alleged, mostly male New York School of poets, or because her recent work shares qualities with that of a younger generation of writers who focus on language play, but because she is so good at what she does. Her poems struck readers from the first as being in some meaningful sense "painterly" —employing "strokes" and "gestures," being occupied with surfaces as much as anything, involving landscapes, interiors, weather, location, etc. I would add to this painterliness the notion of *touch*, with its connotations not solely from painting but also from a great many activities where excellence is a matter of handling and intelligence,

155

i.e., of how and where and not simply what. Look, for example, at what this poet does with observed details in the poems collected in *Moscow Mansions*. Notice how much feeling accompanies the language play of "The Altos." How fresh this way of combining and that way of splitting apart. How relentlessly the newer poems avoid the Scylla and Charybdis of so-called language-centered work, randomness and flatness. I would argue—if pressed—that her own poetic territory, or poetic solution if you like, is one of the genuinely new ones, in contrast to so many allegedly radical rehashings of notions experimented with at least since the '50s and '60s in this country. But this is clearly essay #11 and a big one, and the important thing is that we are the guests, and the poetry table is very high indeed.

LINEUPS II

I wrote the first baseball lineup poem more than twenty years ago for a friend who was struggling with a doctoral dissertation in English. By arranging Major British Poets into a batting order, complete with field positions, I was presenting him with a "dissertation" ready-made. Scrappy Alexander Pope was clearly a lead-off man; Milton played first and batted cleanup; Donne pitched (and won 30 games four times).

That same year I came up with nine more lineups and then published them all in a pamphlet. Actually I must have written sixty, before choosing the ten that meant the most to me—or more accurately, about which I had the strongest intuitions concerning where each "player" hit and played. Throughout, I felt that the real inspiration was Rimbaud, at least I hoped so, especially his "Voyelles," which both deranged and rearranged things, was outrageous as well as beautiful, and made no bones about any of it. I wanted my own de-arrangements to be somehow systematic, the idea being that the entire world could theoretically be located on metaphorical coordinates of batting order and position. So I invented lineups for cities, colors, parts of the body, vegetables, diseases, rooms, etc. Then a few summers ago I found myself fooling around with the idea again, which resulted in the second set, including a hitters lineup that

[Commentary for *Ecstatic Occasions, Expedient Forms,* edited by David Lehman (Michigan U. Press, 1996)]

went the basic premise one better, and an "All-Star" team.

Once after a reading someone I respect complimented me on the three lineups I had included, and then inquired about the "little letters and numbers" following the names. I guess I've always known that these list poems can't possibly make sense to everyone. But for those like me who grew up with indelible feelings and memories connected to baseball, there remains a shape and a tone, a *timbre*, to the very notion of shortstop, as there is a timbre not only to the lead-off and cleanup hitters but even to the #5 and #7 "holes" in the order.

It interested me to recall, while doing the first set, that as a child I had bestowed colors on both vowels and numerals—without feeling that my conviction that 5 was orange and always would be (it still feels that way) had to be everyone's conviction. The individual items that fill the lineups don't, or don't invariably, represent endorsements. They are as often as not the given, the state of the world, though clearly some intuitive selection process involving personal experience as well as tastes was also at work.

A MIDWINTER LINEUP

lf   "Not excepting even the credulous Kraus (see his *De Selbys Leben*), all the commentators have treated de Selby's disquisitions on night and sleep with considerable reserve. This is hardly to be wondered at since he held (a) that darkness was simply an accretion of 'black air,' i.e., a staining of the atmosphere due to volcanic eruptions too fine to be seen with the naked eye and also to certain 'regrettable' industrial activities involving coal-tar by-products and vegetable dyes; and (b) that sleep was simply a succession of fainting-fits brought on by semi-asphyxiation due to (a)."

—Flann O'Brien

ss   "A silence seems a solid thing, shot through with wolfish woe"

—Robert W. Service

rf   "Go back to ya prayin' tomato"

—Big Jule

cf   "Another of de Selby's weaknesses was his inability to distinguish between men and women. After the famous occasion when the Countess Schnapper had been presented to him

[1997; printed in *The World* 54]

(her *Glauben ueber Ueberalls* is still read) he made flattering references to 'that man,' 'that cultured old gentleman,' 'crafty old boy' and so on. The age, intellectual attainments and style of dress of the Countess would make this a pardonable error for anybody afflicted with poor sight but it is feared that the same cannot be said of other instances when young shop-girls, waitresses and the like were publicly addressed as 'boys.' In the few references which he ever made to his own mysterious family he called his mother a 'very distinguished gentleman' (*Lux Mundi* p. 307), 'a man of stern habits' (ibid p. 308) and 'a man's man'..."

—Flann O'Brien

1b   "I may say that only three times in my life have I met a genius and each time a bell within me rang and I was not mistaken, and I may say in each case it was before there was any general recognition of the quality of genius in them. The three geniuses of whom I wish to speak are Gertrude Stein, Pablo Picasso and Alfred Whitehead. I have met many important people, I have met several great people but I have only known three first class geniuses and in each case on sight within me something rang. In no one of the three cases have I been mistaken."

—Gertrude Stein

3b   "To think that, given that we exist, we do not laugh continuously."

—Arthur Cravan

2b   "Though he did not recognise sleep as such, preferring to

160

regard the phenomenon as a series of 'fits' and heart-attacks, his habit of falling asleep in public earned for him the enmity of several scientific brains of the inferior calibre."

—Flann O'Brien

c   "I like a view but I like to sit with my back turned to it."

—Gertrude Stein

p   "The suave blonde is paddling down the skies"

—Clere Parsons

TREVOR WINKFIELD'S PROSE WRITINGS

About a dozen years ago I reviewed a show of Trevor Winkfield's paintings which featured, among other brilliantly wacky creations, a sort of triptych called *Cottage Industries,* which consisted of an elf with a cheerfully demented grin driving a sled in the middle of nowhere, a cardboardish proper Englishman stuck on a peg-like stand and looking heavenward, and a perspiring woodsman sawing a pencil-pointed log while standing on one leg and wearing the first cut for a hat. The title of the show was *Radical Daftness.*

Daft—which is to say in part, displaying an eccentricity we Americans think of as peculiarly English—or not, Winkfield's radically playful, inimitable paintings, book and magazine covers and illustrations, and (almost unknown) poems and prose poems have become a fact of American artistic life. These writings, now collected in *In the Scissors' Courtyard,* were all done between 1967 and 1975, a time when he had temporarily given up painting (a scary thought to his admirers) and was reading and translating Raymond Roussel and editing the exemplary little magazine *Juillard* (which I remember feeling honored to have been invited to contribute to back in 1969). In his work on Roussel and in these writings— which he now regards as "verbal descriptions of future paintings"— he discovered a new way to paint.

The Roussel influence shows up in the writings in his treatment

---

[Introduction at The New School, June 1994]

of the most *un*usual events, conjunctions, and contraptions—zany, enigmatic, and bizarre are just a few of the terms that come repeatedly to mind to characterize them—*as if* they were perfectly normal. Not only are they not normal, they may be profoundly unsettling, unsettlingly amusing, or downright horrifying. Most often they appear arbitrary, without rime or reasons, mysterious as events in the grownup world seem to children, who are the heroes of these tales and whose view of the world predominates. The speaker in one states:"There is no explanation. Or one is not forthcoming." That seems to me to give the atmosphere of Winkfield's Kinderszenen, which are clearly like no one else's. What is unnerving as well as exhilarating is that so many of their components are so familiar—the foods, lost teeth, ghost stories, confusions, magical landscapes, nonstop activity, and relentless brattiness we all grew up with—and yet here everything is out of kilter, unregistered (clearly foreshadowing the paintings in the future) or far worse. Not only is nothing as it would seem to be, but it rarely remains as it was for any time at all. Certainly this is neither Schumann nor Kansas, but neither, somehow, is Kansas Kansas; nor, the book demonstrates, need it be.

Edward Barrett's Preludes

This is an exhilarating book by a poet just about unknown outside the Boston area (excepting a few poets in New York) and published by a tiny, admirable press. It deserves to be known by everybody. Meditations of a particularly wide-ranging (and detecting) sort, Edward Barrett's *Common Preludes* are common in their determined focus on daily experience—rather than aspiring, say, to the condition of music. In many other respects they are rare.

Perversely, I want to call Barrett's work "language poetry," when I know quite well it has virtually nothing in common with the writing that goes by that name. In fact his poems—in both prose and lines—are highly personal (though they expand to become genuinely philosophical and ramify to include large public chunks of the world); "narrative"; brimming with feeling; more often than not formed in some sense (sequences, cadences, openings, closures, syntax, etc.). But they are also *of, for,* and, mysteriously, *by* language itself, which pours forth without stopping (or would if not for the poet's skill in breaking the flow), as though what experience *is*, not to speak of what it may mean, is determined by the language it gives rise to continuously.

That is to say—though how, exactly, remains unclear to me—experience, at least in Barrett's experience, demands to be written about. This is the feeling I get in reading these complex poems cel-

[*Poetry Project Newsletter,* April/May 1996]

164

ebrating the complexities of daily life. Language is on display, but display isn't its function any more than mere recording is. It is more a matter of experience being constituted, at least in large part, by words. Strikingly, *saying*—what should be said, what must be said, what could be said and to whom—is central: "I was saying..." "There isn't much to say about..." "Do you want to say *so much?*" A beautiful evening scene has snow changing from the color of one envelope (i.e., language-holder) to that of another. Two girls say something arresting about a third, and the remark produces and is reproduced in a poem. "It was like a whisper..." "Writing glosses on the violet-blue text of seeming." The poet is somehow the necessary correspondent.

In reality, Barrett is closest to qualifying as a New York Poet, who happens to live and write in New England (and to have a part of his heart in Ireland). Ashbery can be glimpsed behind a tone, or in a question that leaves some puzzlement or perception suspended. One poem is dedicated to Schuyler. The sense of intimacy between poet and reader—who is often the silent participant in a dialogue—evokes O'Hara. But Barrett has his own voice and his own concerns. His feeling for place is especially striking, spots of time relating to Brooklyn or Vermont or the west coast of Ireland; certain slants and shades of light and dark (I discern nocturnes here as well as preludes, also much in the way of impromptu and rhapsody); what stores used to be where; the things a drugstore once sold. Barrett's down-to-earth intellectuality, lyricism, and wit ("Everyone—please—remain calm: take off your wings..." "The important desires are forlornly crazy...") resonate through the book.

Although about half the poems are in lines, prose poems seem to me where Barrett's real sensibility lies. His unit is the paragraph, whether in verse or in prose. The poems in lines have a prose music. I'm tempted to call it the music of intelligence, as one might say of Wallace Stevens—keeping in mind that Stevens is far less earthy, less conversational, more cerebral (necessary angel vs. necessary correspondent).

There are obvious risks when a poet is as fluent as Barrett; yet rarely does the gift for gab take control of a poem rather than the other way around. Mostly the poems convince us that they travel as they do because they are required to do so: chasing down leads, separating nuances, springing sideways in CD-ROM fashion, providing their own connective tissue. "There's this momentum we follow toward what is not in the world and there's no turning back, counting one after the other, translating effects into causes, translating not ignorance but expectation into understanding, regret, exhilaration."

THE INDULGENCE PRINCIPLE

Years ago, I came up with the idea of writing something on "critical fallacies," all the wrong-headed ways critics (reviewers, academics, etc.) approach poetry. I only got as far as making lists of suggestive titles. For one thing, Theory had already reared its head and, in addition to scanting poetry, was busy diverting attention from what I.A. Richards termed practical criticism. For another, I was more interested in writing poems. I almost included a Critical Fallacies Lineup in my second set of *Lineups* (1987), but it didn't make the final cut.

Recently I came across an old notebook list that has, among a lot of others, The Conceptual Fallacy, The Manifest(o) Fallacy, The Development Fallacy, Poetics Justice, The Attention Principle (a few "principles" found their way in: actually this one got mentioned in one of the first prose pieces I ever wrote—on Harold Bloom misprizing John Ashbery), The Da Capo or Sisyphus Principle (after Santayana), The Droll/Jolly/Temperate Principle (after Frank O'Hara), The Exploration/Scientist Fallacy, The Humility Principle, The Designated Hitter (or Managed Care) Fallacy, The Fabergé Fallacy, The Indulgence Principle, The Richard Tuttle Principle, The Principle of Grudging Admiration, The Importance of Being Earnest.

I still find the titles and implicit issues, at least as I perceive them, provocative. One that seems to me basic is the Indulgence Principle, which takes its cue from Pound's observation that "No man

[1996]

writes very much poetry that 'matters.'" Pound doesn't name names, but certain poets rocket to mind, for example Wordsworth, whose handful of great poems shine out against pages upon pages of dull verse, or, even more obviously, Thomas Hardy. Even a poet as self-conscious as Elizabeth Bishop has slight or merely well-crafted poems that are not the reasons her poetry will endure. It's difficult to think of anyone short of Sappho who isn't remembered for that fragment that represents his/her finest, the rest being background: failed experiments, partial successes, unnecessary repetitions, wrong turns, unwitting self-parody: together, the production of an ongoing writing life that proceeds with no advance assurances regarding which efforts will wind up at the top, at the bottom, or in the middle when that writing life is eventually summed up.

Coleridge, in his *Biographia Literaria,* maintains that "our genuine admiration of a great poet is a continuous undercurrent of feeling; it is everywhere present, but seldom anywhere as a separate excitement." Whether this lets Wordsworth, for one, off the hook or not, it does provide ample room for mediocrity and worse. What Coleridge was, of necessity, less aware of than we are is the extent to which poems, together with all the poet's operations and decisions concerning them, have unconscious roots (apart from opium dreams). A poet's attachment to what he/she writes, including judgments about whether to finish a poem, publish it, collect it, etc., is inevitably shrouded in mystery, at least to some degree. However self-conscious, the practitioner side can't be trusted; it has too much unconscious investment in what it produces.

This unconscious factor seems to me a plausible if not entirely satisfying answer to the question, How could someone who wrote *that* have written *this*? Pound goes on to say *(A Retrospect)* that when the poet isn't producing "this highest thing, this saying the thing once for all and perfectly...he had much better be making the sorts of experiment which may be of use to him in his later work, or to his successors." We might say, all well and good if the poet, man or woman, knows when this highest thing is occurring. Experience says otherwise. Allen Ginsberg, asked in an interview how much of his daily note-taking made its way into print, responded, "Oh, one percent." From my own experience that's not so surprising; yet neither is a one percent solution sufficient to ward off the mediocre. There is a reason poets have been visited (or left to palely loiter) by the Muse, and why prayer, for a poet, is appropriate both at the beginning and at the end of a poem.

Not that the experimenting isn't vital. Experience says, at least my experience both reading and writing, that poets *need* to write badly, as well as middlingly and well, in order to produce the "highest thing"—if indeed they are capable of it at all. A part of the writing life, apart from experiment, would seem to be getting lower things out of the system. Another part is ongoing production involving, at its very core, trial and error. Still another involves discovery, even if what is discovered frequently finds its appropriate setting only later on, and in many cases can't be acknowledged as a discovery until then. Poets do learn from their mistakes just as all human beings do; they also continue to make them—and occasionally to avoid them. One of my favorite contemporary poets once related the following anecdote. After writing at fever pitch one evening he felt, quite simply, that he had produced his best poem ever; he had finally *done it*. The following morning he threw it in the basket.

This is one side of the Indulgence Principle: indulging poets the bulk of their (inferior) work in order to have their very best. (Of course, as Eliot would add, only those poets who have a very best

169

deserve indulging.) As such, the principle is an appreciative one, generous without being mindless. Rather than prescribe or exclude, it displays gratitude that certain poems have coalesced out of the welter of language and experience with the power to interest or move us in ways almost no other experience seems capable of.

The other side of the Indulgence Principle is equally important, though less often acknowledged either by critics or by poets themselves. Equally appreciative and generous, this side grants a poet the right not to please a reader in every respect: it recognizes that the "highest thing" is not only rare but inextricable from all the rest. We are used to accepting a writer's or artist's subject matter as given. Accepting certain qualities of style as "givens" is frequently harder. There are, long out of the woodwork by now, many who are put off by John Ashbery's ironic self-indulgence to the degree that they cannot see his originality and importance—indeed, that he is probably the most important poet in English in the second half of the century. Others can't read Faulkner or Henry James and are similarly barred from those writers' brilliances. Among modern poets, Marianne Moore is finical, Auden cerebral (or superficial); Hart Crane emits alcohol fumes; William Carlos Williams has "no ideas"; Laura Riding is "claustrophobic," Bishop control personified; Frank O'Hara (and James Schuyler and David Schubert and John Wheelwright) has a precious streak; Kenneth Koch relies on formulas; Barbara Guest is airy; Robert Creeley is narrowly focused. Among poets of my own generation, friends included, everyone who comes to mind could be said to be this or that, or too this or too that, self-indulgent, self-involved, narrow in range, cerebral, intent on a persona, intent on getting a laugh, determinedly "unserious," eclectic, prosy; and on and on. And yet I have named, and left unnamed, the contemporary poets who matter the most to me.

170

What the Indulgence Principle represents is a willingness to take poems on their own terms, insofar as that is humanly possible. It encourages reviewers and critics (and teachers of poetry, who present poetry to readers in the only place many of them will ever encounter it) to display the reasons why persons not obliged to read poems find some of them such stunning human achievements. In granting poets their blind spots, stylistic tics, excesses, and the like, it doesn't cede the right to find fault, or to dismiss outright the work of those who are merely mediocre or merely imitators. But the judgments made in its name are premised upon appreciation rather than grounds for exclusion. The other approach—I should say approaches—diminish our artistic lives and probably our lives in general, and the Indulgence Principle, if it had the power, would disbar those who fail to take note.